I Never Thought Addiction Could Happen To Me

The 3 Secret Addictions That Are Shattering
the Lives of College Students...
and What to Do About It!

By

LOREE TAYLOR JORDAN

Madison Publishing

Division of LTJ Associates, Inc.

P.O. Box 231

Campbell, CA 95009

(408) 379-9488

Editing & cover design by Dawn Teagarden

ISBN #97809679787811

Library of Congress# 000-00000

Printed in the United States of America

Warning-Disclaimer

The information in this book is for educational purposes only and should not be used to diagnose addiction or treat diseases. If you have a serious health or addiction challenge you should consult a competent health practitioner or doctor. It is your responsibility and privilege to gain knowledge and wisdom about the dangers of addiction so that you may enjoy a clean and sober lifestyle. Educational materials produced by the author's company, LTJ Associates Inc, are an independent effort. The author and publisher shall have neither liability or responsibility to anyone with respect to any loss or damage caused, or alleged to be caused, directly or indirectly by the information contained in this book.

Acknowledgments

I would also like to thank my husband Frankie, who became my hero for his tireless dedication and support efforts in bringing I Never Thought Addiction Could Happen to Me across the finish line. He kept me focused on this book and managed the household with perseverance as a committed team member. I am grateful for his patience on days when I didn't have any!

I want to give special acknowledgment to my incredible mentor and therapist, Joy Sweet, who never ceases to amaze me in all the years that I have worked with her. Her compassionate healing techniques, her validation, and understanding of the core wounds in my soul and that of my family is just beyond comprehension.

My two sons, Brandon and Christopher who through their own painful addictions, and life experiences have shaped who I am today. As we continuously forge ahead to be in healthy relationship with each other we can only take it one day at a time.

I especially want to thank all the recovering addicts who contributed their incredible stories of hope to It Could Never Happen To Me. Their generosity to carry the message to others with cooperative spirit has made this book possible. My wholehearted appreciation goes to everyone who contributed to the lifesaving message of this book.

My dearest friends, Carrie, Gloria, Martha and Nina who are always there for me no matter what!

You are all, truly, the wind beneath my wings.

"Loree doesn't write about addiction she has lived it. She has lived through the destruction of her family of origin, her first marriage and then her son's struggle with drug addiction and incarcerations. *"I never thought addiction could happen to me"* is a powerful book of compassion for any student who may not know yet they are truly dealing with the cunning and deadly disease of addiction."

  — Eddie B. recovering drug addict and former facility Supervisor of
   New Life Recovery Center

"Ms. Jordan should be commended by college administrators. Her book *"I never thought addiction could happen to me"* is taking a huge step forward in addressing the serious issues of compulsive gambling with students as well as other destructive addictions. Whether it's in dorm rooms or at a "casino night" fundraiser, gambling pervades college campuses. Colleges and universities should take on a responsibility to provide information about the dangers of gambling to their students, to think about their own ethics and values, to be sure they understand where they can go for help if they think they might have a problem.

  — Arnie Wexler, Certified Compulsive Gambling Counselor and Past
   Executive Director of the Council on Compulsive Gambling of New Jersey

" Loree Taylor Jordan's book *"I never thought addiction could happen to me"* should get into the hands of every college student. Young celebrity role models that are drinking, using drugs and exhibiting acting out behavior seems to be touted as the normal rite of passage for this age group. The real truth is college students are in severe addiction crisis and they are dying because of it."

  — Irwin Zucker-Publicity Agent Hollywood, CA

"When you read stories like the student at the University of Wisconsin who murdered three roommates because he owed them thousands of dollars in gambling debts, it is bone chilling. As educators we have a moral responsibility to address these addiction issues head on. Bringing Loree's powerful book and life-saving message to college campuses is an absolute MUST!

  — Rosemary Lazetera, Program Assistant of Student Life,
   Evergreen Community College

"Loree Taylor Jordan should be wearing a superhero uniform. Her book is pure power. I can't believe what she's been through and how she uses her super powers to help addicts and the people who love them. The stories in this book are wrappers for even deeper truths. Truths that everyone needs to hear. Thank god Loree Taylor Jordan had the courage to write this book. Read it and give it to someone you love."

  — Linda Hollander aka "Wealthy Bag Lady" author of Bags to Riches,
   empowers young women

Dedication

This book is dedicated to my husband Frankie and both
of my sons Brandon & Christopher. We have all walked
the treacherous journey of addiction to recovery
taking one day at a time!

I have learned so much from each of you
in your own magical way.
I love you!

Table of Contents

Chapter One
A Nightmare Revisited

"Believe that, when you are most unhappy,
there is something for you to do in the world."
— Helen Keller

As the police escorted my son Chris down the hallway, I felt the tears welling up in my eyes; I could hardly look his way. The officer turned to address me. He told me that my son was in possession of chrystal meth. My heart sank. I looked up, saw Chris' hands behind his back, and caught the glistening of metal handcuffs—a picture that stabbed me straight in the heart. It made me drop to my knees, sobbing uncontrollably. I lifted my eyes again and caught Chris' eye. *"Sorry, Mom,"* he said softly, as the cops took him out the front door.

After they had left, I just lay on the floor for about an hour, just sobbing from my gut. This was too much, how much more was I to take? We were so close. We were just hours away from Chris checking himself into a drug rehab. Was this some storyline in Law & Order? No. It's real. My youngest son had been arrested.

What added to the pain was that he had been arrested so many times before. I, in fact, had played this nightmare already. I asked myself: why doesn't it stop, why doesn't *he* stop? It hurts like hell! How could this happen again?

It happened again because my son suffers with the disease of *drug addiction.*

Several Lifetimes with Addiction

The scene that played that day the police took my son away was a scene very familiar to me, and not just because it wasn't the first time Chris had been arrested. I have other versions of this struggle. The names and faces may have been different in the other versions, the dialogue about something else, but the theme is always the same: addiction destroying lives. You see, I have battled addiction from all frontiers: in my personal life as a teen and an adult, as a daughter, as a mother, and as a spouse. I am too familiar with its faces. I personally know how it can destroy lives.

I share this with you so that you can see from my heart where I am coming from. My hope is that through my sharing, I can encourage you to take an honest, perhaps even brutal, look at yourself and those around you. I want to spare you and your family the pain of addiction. If I can get your heart to resonate with mine for a moment, maybe you and I can do something to make sure addiction doesn't affect more lives than it already has.

Let me start at the beginning.

My story starts long before I had Chris, as a child living with a raging alcoholic father and a mother stuck in severe co-dependency[1]. My life script with my parents for the first 16 years of my life was very volatile. When I say volatile, I mean severe, bordering on life threatening—an environment of trauma, physical abuse, and verbal abuse.

One of the most significant events frozen in time in my memory was the night my father physically beat my mother. He had beaten her so badly I thought he was going to kill her. My father, in a drunken rage, had knelt over my mother, and slammed her head into the floor. The blood was everywhere. My sister and I ran to her aid, pulled my father off of her, called the police, and had him removed from the house, guns and all.

[1] maladaptive, compulsive behaviors learned by family members in order to survive in a family which is experiencing great emotional pain and stress caused by a family member's addiction.

My father was a big man, 6 feet tall and weighing over 200 pounds. For two young girls to take him on, in absolute fear and terror, had to be an adrenaline protective reaction. My sister and I were terrified of my father and rightly so; he physically abused us as well. Being hit, slapped, or kicked was as normal in our house as taking out the garbage. If furniture was not flying, it was a slow night.

When I was sixteen years old my mother was diagnosed with breast cancer. In the midst of her trying to save her own life, she finally put an end to a miserable marriage and proceeded with a divorce. My parents were divorcing after 19 years of marriage.

I then had the traumatic experience of seeing my dad pack his belongings and drive away as I stood sobbing at the window. As a teenager I took this all on with fear, guilt, and hurt, as if I had some control over the situation. The truth is, my parents' divorce was not about me, it was about their life unraveling. I was just caught in the circumstances.

Believe me I did not have this all figured out at the time. When my dad was leaving, I was coming apart at the seams watching him drive away. I was in so much emotional pain that I didn't know what to do with myself. I couldn't cry, I couldn't express my emotions. I was frozen inside like a popsicle, but on the outside I looked as if I had it all together. I was outgoing, well liked at school, dating the captain of the football team, and performing well in speech and drama (my favorite subjects). Watching me you would have thought I came from a functional and sane household.

I looked and acted like a normal teenager on the outside. In secret though, I was carrying on an insane life. Just insane, but I needed to cope.

I dealt with it through food.

My Personal Battle with Food Addiction

All of the life-changing events I was living through, and their resulting stress, were just about unbearable for me. I found solace in eating, my drug of choice. Eating was a way to numb my emotions.

Truth is, I would have been better off crying and letting out the feelings that I felt were drowning me instead of trying to show the world I had it all together and eating over it. But it wasn't until many, many years later in counseling, when all the repressed feelings came oozing out in every other aspect of my life, that I was willing to really take a look at the situation and finally understand my feelings about it.

My modus operandi was simple, but potentially deadly. Throughout high school, I gorged on sweets and then starved for days to repent for my sugar sins. I was always waking up from a sugar coma.

My addiction was facilitated by my work at a pizza parlor as a cashier. Since I was able to eat at work for free, I would gorge a pizza around 4:00pm in the afternoon, and then starve until 4:00pm the next day. When I wasn't on this crazy diet, I was eating a school lunch (with Oreos for dessert,) and then going without food for 24 hours until the next day. I was insane with my eating addiction. I could sneak cookies out of the cookie jar with the precision of a brain surgeon!

Two more traumatic events pushed me further into a desire to withdraw from the pain. The first one happened when I was 18 when my mother finally lost her battle to breast cancer. On October 12, 1973, she passed away quietly in her sleep. It was one of the most painful days of my entire life.

The second happened four years later when my infant son, Brandon, was just 2 months old. I was dealt another tragic blow that would change my life forever. I was told that my 64-year-old grandma Tina had been found raped and brutally murdered. My grandmother and I were very close. I cannot begin to describe the pain you feel when you lose someone in such a violent way. The shock is so devastating that it shakes you to the very core of your being. Nothing in the court system can make you feel vindicated, because you can't have your loved one back. You go on wondering how your heart will heal from this tragedy.

It was all too much. I didn't know it at the time, but I was coping with all these traumas by divorcing my emotions from the events happening around me. My eyes and ears perceived what was going on, yes, but my actual feeling about it was frozen. I locked my emotions away, shut and bolted the door. As the days passed I had somehow made myself believe that I had forgotten the event, gotten over it and even dealt with it. Truth was, it all remained inside, simmering underneath the surface. It was still with me, operating at an unconscious level. The hurt, the guilt and the anger were still influencing the choices that I made.

So, aside from an eating addiction, I also got into the diet pill trap. It was easy. Because I worked in a dental office, I had access to controlled substances and I got diet pills through one of the drug companies. This access to supply made me not just a diet pill junkie, but a distributor to my friends as well.

The diet pill abuse made me feel terrible all the time. I was shaky and irritable. If you had looked at me the wrong way back then, I could snap you like a twig. PMS could not hold a candle to me on a diet pill day. I was going days without eating.

I was like an anorexic on speed.

History Repeats Itself

It's ironic; the things you promised you would avoid repeating tend to be the things you end up getting.

Having come from a difficult household, I had no intention of repeating the cycle. But I had found myself later as a young wife in my 20's, raising two young sons with a verbally and physically abusive marriage. I was such an emotional wreck that I would go for days without eating or binge eating and I was very depressed. I finally sought counseling to deal with my emotions of a crumbling marriage.

In counseling, I learned that the past had much to do with the present. Because I have never really explored my feelings growing up, I had yet to move on from my experience as a child of an alcoholic. In fact, I was not even ready yet at that point to accept that an addiction problem existed in my family. My younger sister, Cheryl had started counseling and said to me "you know dad was as alcoholic" and she encouraged me to get help also. My exact words to the therapist in my denial were *"I know my dad drank a lot but he was not an alcoholic."*

But he was, and counseling made me accept this difficult fact. Breaking through this denial was a significant milestone for me. When I did accept that my father had a problem, it was the beginning of my journey to sanity, recovery and learning about the family disease of alcoholism—the disease that had tormented me my whole life.

Through counseling, I understood then how my history with my alcoholic father was a precursor to a codependent marriage with my husband. As a codependent, I could not possibly recognize warning signs of addiction in a future spouse, because I considered it "normal" given the environment I grew up in. As a child of an alcoholic, I would tend to repeat the history that I grew up in. It was at this point that I realized that the man I was married to at the time (my former husband and my boys' father) suffered from alcoholism as well.

I began to go to recovery meetings: OA (Overeaters Anonymous) and Al-Anon (for families of alcoholics) to get help for my eating disorder and my codependency issues with alcoholism. I also began to take my young boys to counseling to teach them about their emotions, feelings, and about addiction. Through counseling, my sons were helped to understand that because of their family's genetic history with alcoholism, they had a 100% chance of becoming alcoholics or addicts themselves if they decided to experiment with alcohol or drugs.

I did the best that I could to make sure that my kids did not go through the same hell I went through. I was resolved to protect them, I participated in 12-step groups, counseling, and tough love meetings; I did everything I could as a responsible parent to avoid the conse-quences of my history. But I had the genetic family disease of addiction fighting me at every turn. My former husband could not help either of his sons even though he did care about them—he couldn't even deal with his own alcoholism. I did what I could to encourage him to get help but he did not choose the path of recovery. For this reason, when the boys were 15 and 16, I decided to divorce him. I sat my boys down and told them I had had enough. It was at this point that my son Brandon said, *"Mom, what took you so long?"* That single question spoke volumes of what he must have been going through within the family the whole time.

After the divorce, the boys lived with me. I cried every day—I mean *every* day! My husband was gone but it was now my children's turn to fall prey into this illness. Their acting out behavior, drinking, drug use, lying, sneakiness, testing my limits and boundaries. If I did not have a program of recovery, a therapist, and a support group to understand the disease of addiction, I would have lost my mind. There were actually many days I thought I had gone insane.

Both of my sons Brandon and Christopher have admitted to experimenting with drugs and alcohol in their early teens and the addiction battle was on. Who would win? Chris who is now 28 admitted to drinking and smoking pot as early as age 12 and being introduced by a friend to chrystal meth at age 14. Brandon now 30 went into rehab at 21 when he was followed into our driveway by the police and issued a DUI, after running red lights then scraping guard rails on a very windy road in the Santa Cruz mountains. He was so inebriated he did not remember how he got home. He was lucky he did not kill himself, the friend he had in the car or anyone else for that matter. I remember holding his clothes and smelling his cologne when he was in rehab and crying out of joy that I at that moment was spared having to bury my son because he had been killed in a drunk driving accident.

At one point when Chris was in one of his many stays in rehab I asked him in family group therapy to accompany me to the funeral home to pick out his casket. That way if I ever got the call to identify his body after a drug overdose I would know what he would want for his funeral. Everyone in the group including Chris was in utter shock that I would be so brutally honest to ask such a thing but this is a brutal reality with drug addiction.

One of my dearest friends (I consider her family) had to go pick up her daughter's body while she was living at college and plan her funeral. She committed suicide after a long battle with a bulimic eating disorder. My friend is so strong but this has been one of the hardest crosses she as ever had to bear losing her precious daughter so tragically as an indirect result of addiction.

This is hard to communicate to you at your age because you are young, have your whole life ahead of you and you don't think addiction or anything like this could *ever happen to you* but parents bury their children every day. I thank God every day that I have not been one of them.

Words can't even begin to express what a long hard painful road this has been in recovery, healing the wounds with my father, losing a marriage and letting go of my former husband, and both my sons' drug & alcohol addictions.

One of the things I wanted so much in life was to be happily married. When I started dating my current husband, Frankie, he smoked pot occasionally and it was a huge issue for us. It started to become a real deal breaker for me but that was just the tip of the iceberg. Little did I know he was keeping a deeper darker secret. He was leading the life of a compulsive gambler, betting on sports events.

I knew something wasn't right many times in my gut but this addiction got past me in the beginning because you can place a bet on a cell phone or online in just a few minutes in secrecy. There are no visible physical signs, red eyes, slurred speech or anything else to let on about this secret addiction if you don't have access to a person's phone records or bank accounts etc. What guy doesn't like to watch sports right?

Later in this book my husband will be sharing his personal story of recovery from drug addiction and his sports betting gambling career that started while in college. My son Chris will share with you in his own words his personal struggle with his chrystal meth addiction, his prison incarcerations and what his life is like now.

The core message of this book without judgment or blame is addiction is a treatable illness *not a moral weakness* and there is hope!

As I open my heart and those that have shared their personal experiences, feelings and struggles, we are real human beings living with addiction either with someone we love or in our own lives. Even though we don't know you personally we do care and we are all here to share our experience, strength and hope.

Welcome to the journey, my friend. Welcome home!

Chapter 2
What is Addiction?

"Don't make any difference if I end up alone,
I'd rather have myself and smoke my homegrown"
— Grammy Winner Jazz Artist Amy Winehouse, "Addicted"

Whenever I speak about addiction to young people like you, my greatest challenge is correcting perception about the gravity and the urgency of this issue. After all, the facts about alcohol and drug use, as well as many other self-defeating behaviors, are readily available. These facts are accessible via the internet, integrated in the school curriculum, and at times even explained on television. Half the time these are things that you already know from somewhere. But whether or not this information would be taken seriously is another matter. Popular culture appears to operate on a split-level consciousness about addiction. On one hand, it is condemned; on the other, addiction is glorified.

Just take a look at pop music for example. Researchers from the University of Pittsburg School of Medicine, led by Dr. Brian Primack, studied 279 of Billboard's Most Popular Music of 2005. They found that *one out of every three songs* glorified drugs or alcohol. The researchers also calculated that American teens (aged 15 to 18) listen to 2.4 hours of music daily and hear 84 musical references to substance use a day—and more than 30,000 a year![1]

And while this rate was based on the music of 2005, it is a safe

1 Primack BA, Dalton MA, Carroll MV, Agarwal AA, Fine MJ. A content analysis of substances of abuse in popular music. Archives of Pediatric and Adolescent Medicine. 2008;162:169-175.

bet that the rate is as high, if not higher, today. Now, with this kind of "normalcy" associated with drug and alcohol use, it is not surprising that it is often perceived as a crisis people tend to exaggerate.

In fact, it is also not unusual for the word "addicted," and related words, to find themselves thrown about casually in everyday language. I am *"addicted"* to this television show; she makes me *"high"*; I need a chocolate *"fix"*,etc. You might consider out–of–control behaviors from our celebrities as entertainment—train wrecks you can't keep our eyes off. You'd be hard-pressed these days to find a youth-oriented show that does not mention alcohol and drug use. Yes, you are used to a casualness about addiction-related concepts that makes it twice as hard to appreciate that this world has a much grimmer side to it.

Language, after all, captures attitudes; it represents ideas. With this kind of permissiveness it is not unusual that when you hear addiction concepts, you do not think about ugly pictures of overdose, young people who have died (or have killed others) via drunk driving at 18 and families ripped apart by emotional and physical abandonment— *well*, unless they happen to be current news. You might give little credence to the horror of waking up on a dangerous street with no idea how you got there, the rate you may be destroying your internal organs each week, or of the possibility that you would one day find yourselves not thinking twice about committing a criminal offense to sustain your addictions. These things are worst-case-scenarios. They are so far away, happening to someone else, happening to less than 1% of the population—*"it will never happen to me."*

It CAN happen to you. It may even be happening to you RIGHT NOW.

> *"One often learns more from ten days of agony*
> *than from ten years of contentment.*
> —*Merle Shain*

Things Are Not Always What They Seem

"Young people share a fundamental unhappiness with their world and a strong desire to work for change, but they doubt deeply that they would do better than their parents did...."
—Henri Nouwen

When you look around your campus, how many people do you see with an easygoing attitude and carefree expression? How many students do not seem to have any serious problems at all?

In the previous chapter, I shared with you about my own unaffected front despite everything that was going in my life back in high school. I kept a happy face to give the appearance to the world that I was all right. But that's what it all is, a front, a mask.

Having made the rounds among other young people during speaking engagements, I know that many other young people are the same—they are different on the inside than how they appear on the outside. I have met plenty of young people who begin our conversations with *"you know, I have never told anyone this, but..."* It makes you think: if I take the time to just ask how others are around me, and they can trust me enough, how many would I find have stories that are different from their masks?

I remember this architecture major named Alec, who when I met him, was in his sophomore year. He was a charming young man, had a great sense of humor (albeit a rather sarcastic one), and active within the student body. He was bright too and has never been known to miss a single day in class. Having come from a relatively affluent family, he seemed to be living a rather charmed life.

What few people knew is that he had been, for years now, living with a verbally and physically abusive parent. He has never told this to anyone; he felt that the best way to handle his problems is to compartmentalize his life into two mutually exclusive categories: home hell and school escape. He felt that good grades and college buddies would compensate for the difficulty that he was going through at home and felt the need to prove to himself that there was at least one area of his life that is going well.

You cannot, however, keep aspects of your life in neat little categories forever. Sooner or later you are going to feel one area of your life spill into the other. True enough, Alec eventually felt the stress from home wearing him down in school: he was failing one subject after another and he was losing interest in all the extra-curricular work that he had pursued before. How can you be enthusiastic about life when you see it devalued everyday? With school achievements no longer a solace; Alec needed another escape route. Sadly, he found his comfort through the abuse of cocaine. No one had been the wiser until Alec was arrested for possession.

Isn't it striking how appearances can be so deceiving? It never fails to surprise me, this guy, if you saw him, looks like an average Joe; he smiles, he jokes around, and he hangs out with buddies. He dresses well and neatly; he is polite to people. You would not be able to guess how much he is carrying emotionally just by looking at his face. Thankfully he had been reached just in time—the arrest jolted him awake to what he was doing to himself and he volunteered for counseling—for he confessed that he was angry enough to even have contemplated suicide.

Let me share with you another story of a young man named Tyler. He was a student who, from the outside, appears brimming with potential—he had good grades and his whole future was right ahead of him. Not known to all, because of addiction, he had found himself doing things that even he does not understand. This story is related by his uncle.

From Straight A's to Family Thief

As I reach for the phone at midnight my heart is pounding as I anticipate the call that every family member dreads: there has been a bad accident. I am stunned as I am told that Tyler my 18-year-old nephew had been hit by a car. He was in a drug-induced stupor as he walked into a four-lane highway of traffic, was hit and flipped into the driver's car that hit him. He was on his way to the hospital. How did everything with Tyler, the little boy that I had come to love, go so terribly wrong?

As a young boy Tyler was my buddy and I thoroughly enjoyed him and we were very close. As a freshman he began to excel in reading, and we discussed many writers. He loved his schoolwork from sophomore to junior year and he scored high on SAT tests. Well that was to take a dramatic turn.

Tyler started smoking pot at probably age 15 but he still managed to keep it all together in school. We had several conversations about the dangers of drugs especially the harder drugs. Tyler assured me that he would never ever use those type of drugs. But as pot lost its magic he did in fact start to use the other drugs out there.

Tyler started using cocaine, speed and OxyContin (synthetic heroin) upping his dependence and usage to a higher level. Since he had already used and became dependant on OxyContin the next step was injecting heroin. Somewhere along the line Tyler stepped over the line from drug usage or experimentation into full-blown drug addiction.

Things went from bad to worse in our family when Tyler started to deal drugs to support his habit. One day some ruffians came to the door and freaked out his parents. They began to realize that his drug problem was getting serious. His parents took him for drug testing. The first test showed cocaine and speed.

His parents tried to get him to go to rehab but he refused to go. At one point his parents kept him basically on house arrest to help him detox for 3 weeks. He got so sick he finally 'fessed up to the doctor that it was heroin. His parents were somewhat in denial that this drug problem had gotten so serious and that he could not kick it with their help nor did he want their help.

Tyler began stealing from the family to support his habit. He stole some of his grandma's jewelry that was living there at the house, his younger sisters I-Pod and then the ultimate insult he figured out electronically how to steal 3,000 out of his parent's bank account. When the bank account theft was discovered and he refused treatment Tyler's parents kicked him out. That was it.

Even though his parents kicked him out they were worried and his father was tracing him through his cell phone. His father took off work to follow him. Even though he was out on the street I believe that Tyler thought his parents would rescue him if the going got really tough.

Then the Sacramento police came to his parent's door one day because they had seen Tyler's license number fleeing a murder scene at a drug house. It turns out that he had been at that location but left before an altercation where a gal was shot and killed.

Tyler was living in a drug house with dealers that were all selling drugs. He called me one night and I picked him up but he was higher than a kite. We were always close I thought I could have a positive influence over him to get help. He kept telling me that he had it all under control he could get out of this drug mess himself. Tyler had not talked with his parents. I encouraged him to at least tell his parents that he was okay and I took him home.

He asked to stay at home. He and his parents came to an agreement about rules but he really didn't keep them, Tyler wanted it his way, to live in his parent's house, have a roof over his head and keep using drugs. He was out of control and becoming a danger to the whole family especially grandma.

I confronted him about his addiction and he got very confrontational. I told him that the family had found a rehab we could take him right now. He fought all of us tooth and nail. He ran out the door his father running after him. As hard as it was his father told Tyler you are out of here it is a rehab program or nothing.

Tyler still chose not to go to rehab.

Tyler did graduate high school we don't know how. He had been accepted to several 4-year colleges but don't know at this point if he is eligible. The week after graduation his brother Rick was coming back from a friend's house saw what he thought was a highway patrol check point. Right then Rick got a phone call from his parents saying that Tyler was hit by a car right where he was. The check point was actually his brother's accident. Tyler's backpack was full of drugs. Tyler had approximately 10 different drugs in his system when he walked across a four-lane highway at night into oncoming traffic. It flipped him through the windshield into the driver's car. Because 911 was immediately called and he was about a mile from a hospital it probably saved his life. He was so full of drugs that they had to wait for a day and half before attempting surgery to reset his arms and legs with titanium rods. He did not even know about the accident when he woke up. He was in the hospital 9-10 days it is a miracle that he even survived. As he was physically recovering at home his brother found a way to watch him on his computer and cell phone and Tyler was still making drug contacts. I wish I could tell you that Tyler was so shaken about almost losing his life and that he agreed to go to rehab to turn his life around. I can't… He is in the grip of an unyielding addiction and only he can decide when enough is enough.

How did you feel reading Tyler's story? Did you feel sad for him? Did you feel mad at him? You may be thinking to yourself, how can one be so smart and make one wrong choice after another? How can one observe his own life fall into pieces around him and still refuse to get help?

But that is the dynamic of addictions. It takes on a life of it's own and Its spirals out of control so that you can't read warning signs—until it is too late.

Now ask yourself: Can the things said about Alec and Tyler be also said about me? Are there several things happening inside me right now that those around me do not know? Is there something that is too painful for me to share and maybe even rather shameful to admit? It may not be something emotionally intense but it can be something that affects you in a significant way. It may even be boredom or a sense of lack of direction. Am I coping with it through an addiction? Am I using a substance or a behavior to medicate myself? Do I still have an objective view of where I am taking my life?

> *"The battle to keep up appearances unnecessarily, the mask–whatever name you give creeping perfectionism robs us of our energies.*
> *—Robin Worthington*

Addictions Numb feelings

Defining addiction is not always a straightforward exercise. There is no one accepted definition of addiction; it often depends on the orientation of the person that you are talking to. Traditionally though, addiction is considered as a *"compulsive physical and psychological need for a substance or behavior."*

A key word in this definition is the word "compulsive." This term implies that in addiction, a behavior is indulged in without the control of the person; your ability to choose has become impaired. When you feel *compelled* to do something, it feels as if the action cannot be resisted; it has to be done over and over again. It has to obeyed, otherwise you will feel anxiety. You cannot just simply say "no."

The compulsive nature of addiction may be traced to unacknowledged internal struggles. You feel compelled to engage in an addiction because without something to occupy your mind, you would be left alone with yourself. When a person is undergoing emotional pain, or is bored and restless, being alone with one's self is a very difficult thing to experience. Thus you would need something to numb yourself from the anxiety that you are feeling.

When analyzed therefore, addictions are actually a way to survive and a way to cope. They are however dysfunctional coping ways and they do not really solve anything. In fact, they even cause more severe problems. But they are anchored to emotional needs that are very real and very much felt by the person.

This dynamic is embedded in the origins of the word. Addiction comes from the word *addicere* which means to *"attach one's self to, to surrender or to give one's self to a habit."* It is therefore tantamount to giving away your power over yourself and letting something else *outside of you* decide how you act, how you feel and how you behave at any particular point in time. It's like giving control of yourself to another person to do with what they wish.

Think of it this way: emotionally healthy people are those who are 100% present in everything that they do. Their attention is not divided; they are able to say that there is no better time than the present and no better place than where they are at any given time. They view life realistically: not in ways colored by anything that has occurred in the past or fears for what will occur in the future. Their reactions befit their situation, they don't overreact nor do they underreact. They are able to profit from every experience, responding to life in a rational and non-emotional (note: not emotionless!) manner. This is your ideal; you want to be (a) open to what is happening outside of you and (b) open to what is happening inside of you.

But when you surrender yourself to an addiction, you dilute this 100% presence in what you are doing. You allow yourself to be distracted. You let go of a part of your ability to direct your life.

This concept of surrender is not that difficult to appreciate. Everyday you might already do this in small doses. For example, when you get absorbed in a movie you are watching, what you are actually doing is temporarily setting aside the present world and allowing yourself to be distracted for a while. The same thing happens when you postpone a homework assignment you don't want to do and surf the net instead, you are re-focusing your attention to the computer from the unpleasant task at hand. When go you get a hair-cut after a broken heart, you are letting your feelings be soothed by something that gives you pleasure.

Well, it's great if from time to time if you can allow yourself to 'escape' reality for a few moments. It helps you maintain your sanity because life can get very difficult and stressful. But imagine these short and temporary escapes magnified several times over. What if instead of letting yourself be taken to another place for a few hours on occasion, you can do it often and for longer periods of time and without any sort of inhibition? What if you let this surrender of personal control become your automatic response to life? What if you can surrender yourself to something else permanently?

Indulging in an "escape" in extreme proportions is what defines addiction. It's being in a moment and yet not being there at all. When this always happens, can we find the time to just be still? Do we still know even how to be alone with ourselves?

"Why everything that's supposed to be bad make me feel so good? Everything they told me not to is exactly what I would"
— Millionaire Producer and Rap Artist
Kanye West, "Addiction"

The Many Faces of Addiction

Most people, when they think about addiction, they think only of drugs and alcohol. But addictions are not limited to these substances. The object of an addiction can actually be anything at all! It can even be something that, if used in moderation, might be socially acceptable, such as work in the case of workaholics. As long as a substance or a behavior is being used to still a feeling of unease (or dis-ease)/ anxiety/ a lack of love and security inside of you, it can be an object of addiction.

How do you know that you are addicted to something? The following elements are said to be cardinal signs of addictions:

"He looked at everything as the cause of his unhappiness–except alcohol."
—Big Book of Alcoholics Anonymous

"One doesn't recognize in one's life the really important moments–not until it's too late."
—Agatha Christie

Obsession

Obsession means that the desire for the object of the addiction is repeatedly in your mind. As you go through every day activities, think of nothing but your addiction. Your addiction takes priority over and above all things. It is a behavior that seems compelled from within and eventually requires that life would revolve around the addiction, so much so that adjustments would be made in a person's schedule just to accommodate an addiction.

Persistence Despite Negative Consequences

Since the addict feels compelled to follow his obsession, an addiction *always* has negative consequences. Often these negative effects are in areas of school and work performance, relationships with people, and even threats to health and life. A sure sign of addiction is the persistence of a behavior despite negative consequences— and despite best efforts to change and best intentions! Even if addicts acknowledge that something is not good for them, they will always find an excuse to continue on participating in this behavior.

Loss of Control

This involves an inability to stop and manage the behavior. When an individual makes specific plans about how much he or she is going to indulge in a substance or behavior on a particular occasion but fails to stick to those plans, he or she is experiencing a loss of control. It is the object of the addiction, e.g. the beer or the drug, that is now more powerful than the person's self-control.

Loss of control is related to the concept of *dependency*. Dependency is different from abuse of a substance; it is a more serious disease. Abuse is a pattern of excessive use of a substance that brings about negative consequences such as health problems or inability to attend fully to work or relationships. There is an experienced difficulty in reducing use and intake despite negative consequences. When you exceed the dose of a drug more than you need for example, or when you take something that you have no prescription for, then you are abusing that drug. Abuse is often a precursor to dependency.

A person is dependent or addicted however when his use of a substance or engagement in a behavior is already met by *tolerance*. Tolerance means that you have to increase dosages of a substance or frequency of a behavior in order to get the same effect, like a "high." Our bodies can get "immune" to a drug or substance and it will not respond to the drug similarly in succeeding tries. Thus you are sucked into a cycle of "chasing the thrill." Continually increasing the dosage to get the same benefit that you are used to.

When you have developed a tolerance already to an object of addiction, any attempt on your part to stop the addiction would be met by *withdrawal symptoms*. These can be physical symptoms like shaking and vomiting, or emotional symptoms like crankiness and mood swings, that signal that your body has begun to 'need' the object of addiction.

Denial

Addictions are characterized by denial. No addict will admit that he has a problem, after all who wants to admit that they do not have control over their life? Thus an addict will try to maintain the illusion that he is still in charge. He may deny by saying explicitly that he has no problem or by not accepting the gravity of the situation. Denial is the main reason why addicts refuse help.

Examples of common denials are: *"I can stop if I want to," "I am just a social drinker," "It's my life," "It doesn't affect anyone else,"* and *"I am entitled to have fun."*

Progression

And lastly, addictions are progressive diseases; there is no other way to go but from bad to worse. The more you indulge in your addiction, the more its consequences will explode in your face in incredible proportions. You will do things that you don't want to do, things you never imagined that you'd do. Addiction will take its toll on your body, if left untreated addictions can become fatal.

Winning the war against addiction starts with awareness. It starts with understanding what addiction really is, how it manifests itself, and what you can do to prevent and overcome it. Specifically, I want to talk to you about the common addictions that affect the lives of college students such as yourself: alcohol, drugs, eating disorders, and compulsive gambling.

"The causes of the drinker's desperate need for escape through alcohol aren't easily explained, even by the trained psychiatrist. We must accept the fact that the alcoholic suffers from a sickness. The family may be able to help him to want sobriety, by changing its way of thinking and acting. Let me free myself from the illusion that I can do anything directly to conquer the disease from which the alcoholic suffers. I need not suffer from another's illness, if only I am willing to accept help for myself. This indirectly helps the alcoholic."
—One day at a time—Al-anon

Chapter Three

I Just Want to Chill Out Have a Brew What's the Problem?

I started drinking at the tail end of high school. My name is Valerie and for me, taking my first drink was a Eureka! moment...it was like I had finally found what was missing in life. I had never been comfortable in my own skin. I was painfully shy and alcohol allowed me to relax and become comfortable around other people.

Things really took off in college. At the time, the drinking age was 18, so when I turned 18 in November, a group of my new friends (drinking buddies) thought it would be funny if I drank a whole bottle of rum. I was drinking rum and cokes about 9/10 rum and 1/10 coke. That night we had a fire drill in the dorm and I had to be carried down eight flights of stairs.

I was already beginning to notice that there was something different about the way I drank compared to other people. To most of my college buddies, partying was something they did for fun. For me, it was something I was compelled to do, pretty much all the time. I challenged myself to function with hangovers by drinking in the morning. I frequently became falling down drunk to the point other people were embarrassed to be seen with me. I was sometimes left at nightclubs by so-called friends.

The first person to notice I had a problem was my college tennis coach. Tennis was very important to me in high school. I was most valuable player of my high school team; my first job was as a tennis instructor. I played on the team in college, but my game was already starting to slip. One day my college tennis coach pulled me aside and asked me if I was having a problem with drugs. I didn't know alcohol was a drug, so I said no.

Alcohol became so important to me that absolutely everything that competed with alcohol had to go. That included friends, boyfriends, competitive tennis and eventually school. I dropped out of school halfway through my sophomore year. I had no plans for my future. I simply quit. I had no motivation to do anything but drink. My life revolved around which nightclubs had what drink specials.

I was already aware that I had a big problem. I was 20 years old. I couldn't hold a job for more than a month or two. I had heard of Alcoholics Anonymous, but thought I was too young to go. So I continued this downward spiral for another eight years. I ended up married to another alcoholic when I was 23. All we had in common was that we were a couple of drunks. Neither one of us could hold a job, but I could hold one for a month or two – he could only hold one for a week or two, so I decided that he had a problem with alcohol and sent him to AA while I continued to drink. Needless to say, it didn't work for him trying to go to AA and coming home to a drunk wife.

In the mean time, I got pregnant and had to quit drinking because of that. I became very ill with asthma and pneumonia and almost died. As soon as I had my daughter, I was back to drinking every day, but by then, I was sure my husband was the problem, and I looked for a way to get out of the marriage. For one thing, while I was pregnant, I was so ill I was physically *unable to work and he refused to work. He wanted to sit by my bedside and watch me die, I guess. We ended up on welfare. I was so humiliated. I had come from an upper middle class family; I had thrown away a ton of opportunity including a college education and here I was living in a tenement run by a slumlord complete with cockroaches and mice married to someone who wouldn't get a job.*

When my daughter was 18 months old, we were divorced. My alcoholism really took off then. I was down to about 89 pounds; I didn't eat, I just drank. I remember one year there was a threat of a hurricane and while people were stocking their homes with food and other supplies, I was going from one liquor store to another stocking my house with booze, terrified of running out, and not wanting anyone to know how much I was really drinking. More about Valerie later....

Reasons Why Alcohol is Socially Acceptable

A student-killer that hides in plain sight is alcohol. It is the most commonly abused substance among college students, even more so than tobacco. According to the College Health Association, it is the single greatest risk to the health of university students.

It is easy to understand why this may be so. For one, unlike other commonly abused drugs, alcohol is probably the easiest to obtain. It is advertised in all forms of media. Alcohol is sold legally in a great variety of places; in fact even the convenience stores have them alongside groceries. In your own neighborhood, you can find liquor stores within 20 miles of each other in any stretch of road. Compared to other drugs, alcohol is also relatively more affordable; right within a college student's budget.

Second, alcohol use is a socially acceptable behavior. You your-self may be thinking right now, what is so wrong with a little beer now and then? Isn't a little alcohol even good for the heart? There is a very little stigma associated with drinking, and you can drink in public without getting raised eyebrows. In fact, there are even contexts like spring break, celebrations and night outs when drinking is expected and to *not* drink is atypical. This makes it twice as hard to clearly delineate between moderate use, abuse and dependency.

Third, some cultural norms consider drinking as the hallmark of adulthood. In fact 'getting to college' may even be considered by some parents as the cut-off point when restrictions on alcohol intake can be lifted. It is associated with "maturity" and "autonomy" which are very attractive to young people starting out to prove their inde-pendence.

Alcohol use is part of many a collegiate rite of passage. In Princeton University for example, alcohol is on tap 24 hours a day, 7 days a week at the eateries. Princeton reunions boast the second highest level of alcohol consumption for any event in the country after the Indianapolis 500. The social norms for drinking at the university are clear: Students must be comfortable with alcohol use to partake of Princeton social life.[1]

It is also an accepted seal of friendship and camaraderie. If you do not drink, you are not one of the "guys" or one of the "girls." You have to be able to take at least one drink for the team. It is for this reason that fraternity or sorority membership is a significant risk factor for college drinking.

With these things in consideration, it is not surprising that alcohol use and abuse among students is very popular.

1 Prentice, D.A. & Miller, D.T. (1993). Pluralistic Ignorance and Alcohol Use on Campus: Some Consequences of Misperceiving the Social Norm. Journal of Personality and Social Psychology 64(2), 243-256.

Binge Drinking

A common practice in campuses is that of binge drinking, defined as having five or more drinks on a single occasion within a two-week period. One survey of students from 140 colleges showed that 44% of students were binge drinkers and 19% were considered frequent binge drinkers. Binge drinkers, particularly frequent binge drinkers, are those often at risk for alcohol-related problems. An interesting finding is that college students have a higher rate of drinking than those of similar age who do not attend college. It seems the college experience creates more risks for alcoholism.[2]

Binge drinking has been known to have considerable effects on a student's academic life; studies have found it statistically related to a lack of motivation in college, whether it is not showing up to class or not studying for a test. In fact, those who binge drink are eight times more likely to miss a class than those who do not. These common habits of binge drinkers can also lead to lower grade point averages.[3] During college, binge drinking may be associated with mental health disorders such as compulsiveness, depression or anxiety, or early deviant behavior.[4]

The commonly abused alcoholic drinks among students include beer, scotch, tequila, vodka, and gin.

Myths and Illusions Related to Alcohol Use

You can play "hunt the urban legend" with student beliefs about alcohol. The popularity of alcohol in campuses is also related to the various myths and illusions associated with drinking. It is best to take

2 Wechsler H, Davenport A, Dowdall G, Moeykens B, & Castillo S. (1994). Health and behavioral consequences of binge drinking in college: A national survey of students at 140 campuses. JAMA. 272(21):1672-1677.

3 Wechsler, H., Dowdall, G., Maenner, G., Gledhill-Hoyt, J. and Hang Lee. (1998). Changes in binge drinking and related problems among American college students between 1993 and 1997: Results of the Harvard School of Public Health College Alcohol Study, Journal of American College Health, Volume 47.

4 National Institute on Alcohol Abuse and Alcoholism (1995). College Students and Drinking, Alcohol Alert No. 29, Bethesda, MD: U.S. Department of Health and Human Services.

stock of them and see you subscribe to them in anyway. Subscribing to these myths can cost you your life.

Below are some of the rationizations that relate to alcohol and the facts to debunk them:

"All my friends drink anyway."

"It was my roommate who got me into drinking. She and her friends go out every night with high school buddies and do not go back home until early in the morning. I figured, if she does it, why shouldn't I, right?"

The greatest influence for alcohol use in colleges are peer groups. Because we are often far from home at this stage in our lives, we spend the majority of the day with our friends. Aside from giving us company and support as we go through our classes, they also help us discover who we are independent of families. It would be difficult to survive college life if you do not have any friends at all.

The acceptance of peer groups are very important to us. Whether consciously or unconsciously, we measure our worth based on how others see us. Their opinions matter to us, especially if they are people we admire and value. Our friends serve as mirrors to tell us if we are alright, if we are fitting in or deviating badly from the rest.

No one in his right mind wants to be rejected. It is a painful thing to go through, more so if it is not the first time that you have experienced abandonment. Thus for most of us, it is within second nature to do a little "social connection" when we are in the company of others. You first survey silently what the rest may be endorsing before you form your own opinion. You might conform to the perceived standards in order to be one of the 'guys' or 'girls.' Peer groups therefore are believed to figure significantly in whether or not occasional drinking will get integrated into the lifestyle of a student.

Is it true though that everyone drinks in college? You'd be surprised. Recent studies show that a positive attitude to drinking is not as universal as students assume. In Prentice and Miller's study of college students' drinking attitude and behavior, for example, it was found that students tend to overestimate the university norm and adjust their own behavior based on this overestimate. Prentice and Miller asked students to rate their own comfort level with college drinking practices on a scale of 1 to 10 with 10 as the most comfortable. On the average, students rated themselves with a 4, indicating that in private they are not as comfortable as they present themselves to be. But when asked to rate their friends' comfort level with campus alcohol practices, as well as the average students', they rate them a 7 out of 10! It's funny, but this actually implies that most students see themselves as more conservative than the rest. Now when these perceptions were related with actual behavior, it was found that it is the opinion of the norm rather than the self that influences what a student would end up doing. This is more so among the guys, who tend to shift their attitudes to the perceived norm to avoid campus alienation.[5]

This implies that alcohol use is not as pervasive as you might think it is, and there may just be merit to your own private opinion. Perhaps you are just most sensitive to public displays of drinking and presume that everyone feels the same way. But it is certainly not true that if you feel like abstaining from or managing your alcohol, you are somewhat of a freak.

"Alcohol is a Stress Reliever"

Many drink because they claim that drinking relaxes them. After a long hard day or a particularly busy afternoon, it feels good to just sit back and relax with a bottle.

That alcohol can be a stress-reliever has some truth to it. Alcohol

5 Prentice, D.A. & Miller, D.T. (1993). Pluralistic Ignorance and Alcohol Use on Campus: Some Consequences of Misperceiving the Social Norm. Journal of Personality and Social Psychology 64(2), 243-256.

is a drug; it is a kind of depressant. Depressants are substances designed to relieve tension, irritability and anxiety. In moderation, it can be an effective way to iron out the kinks brought about by the day.

It is not a cure-all, however, and it is NOT TRUE that the more you drink, the more relaxed you'd feel. It is not a way to forget your problems either. Alcohol does not relieve stress by lessening your feeling of tiredness and removing the source of stress your life. Rather, alcohol works by impairing your brain's ability to perceive things properly. You feel less problematic not because the problems are gone but because alcohol intake affects your ability to attend to the problem. It restricts your ability to process your experience. Meanwhile, the problem may just be getting bigger and bigger and you cannot see it.

"I am not hurting anybody."

"What harm can a few drinks do, anyway?"

Because alcohol is tolerated by society, the most common misconception is has no negative effects associated with it.

Far from a victimless crime, alcohol use and abuse have the power to destroy both the person drinking and the people around them—especially those that they love. The more you indulge, the more likely you will get addicted. And as you go along this path, the repercussions become worse and worse.

Straight up, alcohol abuse is FATAL. Excessive drinking is like building repositories of waste inside your body. Long term effects of substance abuse on the body include: liver diseases like liver hepatitis, liver cancer; cirrhosis; digestive system problems like gastritis, stomach-bleeding; ulcers, malnutrition; cardio-vascular diseases like high blood pressure; enlarged heart, and increased risk for stroke. It is also responsible for problems in the nervous system like brain atrophy-loss of brain tissues, distorted thinking, hallucinations, dementia, delirium, and seizures.

And it is not just alcohol's direct effects on health that you ought to be worried about. Chew on these statistics for a moment. Every year, 1,700 college students between the ages of 18 and 24 die each year from alcohol-related unintentional injuries, including motor vehicle crashes while 599,000 students between the ages of 18 and 24 are unintentionally injured. More than 696,000 students between the ages of 18 and 24 are assaulted by another student who has been drinking annually and more than 97,000 students between the ages of 18 and 24 are victims of alcohol-related sexual assault or date rape.

Risk-taking behavior also increases with alcohol intake. Four hundred thousand students between the ages of 18 and 24 had unprotected sex after drinking and more than 100,000 students between the ages of 18 and 24 report having been too intoxicated to know if they consented to having sex. Between 1.2 and 1.5 percent of students indicate that they tried to commit suicide within the past year due to drinking or drug use. More than two million students between the ages of 18 and 24 drove under the influence of alcohol. This is especially alarming because as the blood alcohol level of a binge drinker increases, their risk of crashing is almost up to nine times more than someone who is driving the legal limit (Federal Office of Road Safety. 2004).

"I can drink and still be in control."

Others have minimized the effect of alcohol in the body because they claim that it doesn't affect them strongly enough that they lose the ability to be in command of themselves. In fact they even argue that alcohol gives them more control over themselves—they become more courageous after a few drinks. An understanding of our own biology can easily debunk this myth.

Alcohol and the Human Body

Absorption

Alcohol is primarily absorbed through the stomach and the small intestines. It is considered a food because it has calories, but does not need to be digested and proceeds directly into the body through the digestive system. After ingestion it is carried through the blood stream and crosses the blood-brain barrier, at which time impairment begins. A greater amount of ingestion causes greater impairment to the brain, which, in turn, causes a person to have a greater degree of difficulty in functioning.

Metabolism/Elimination

The majority of alcohol in the body is eliminated by the liver. Ninety percent is eliminated through the body, while ten percent is eliminated (unchanged) through sweat and urine. Before the liver can process alcohol, a threshold amount is needed and can occur at the rate of one 12 oz. can of beer, on 5 oz. glass of wine, or $1\frac{1}{2}$ oz. shot of whiskey per hour. When the alcohol content in the bloodstream (the blood alcohol level) is about 0.1 percent (the equivalent of drinking 5 ounces of whiskey or 5 glasses of beer), the muscular coordination is also impaired. The drinker may have trouble walking a straight line and pronouncing certain words. At the 0.5 percent blood alcohol level, the person may loose consciousness and even die.

Short-term Effects

Reduces sensitivity to pain loss of inhibition, poor judgment and reduced concentration.

Affects vision in the following ways: narrows the visual field, reduces resistance to glare, interferes with the ability to differentiate intensities of light, and lessens sensitivity to colors.

Long-term Effects

Damage to vital organs; including liver, heart and pancreas

Linked to served medical conditions; including gastro intestinal problems, malnutrition, high blood pressure, and lower resistance to disease. Also, linked to several types of cancer, including esophagus, stomach, liver, pancreas and colon.

Alcoholism

Tolerance, as discussed earlier, can easily progress alcohol use and alcohol abuse to alcoholism. Alcoholism is a disease. It has identifiable symptoms, identifiable progression, and treatment. The craving that an alcoholic feels for alcohol can be as strong as the need for food or water. An alcoholic will continue to drink despite serious family, health, or legal problems. Because of this he is no longer just a person choosing something that he wants to do with his life, but rather he is ill needing intervention.

Often, alcoholism starts with experimentation. This may be brought on by simply curiosity or boredom. For the average American, experimentation with alcohol occurs during high school, with peer groups. It will later progress to social and recreational drinking which includes moderate drinking for self-enjoyment.

It is often at social drinking stage that young people discover that drinking can be used to medicate yourself. It is a constant way to relieve one's self of whatever emotions, feelings or situations that you are uncomfortable with. When drinking follows a pattern of use already, alcohol use has progressed to abuse. Meanwhile the body's tolerance has increased.

Six months of continuous alcohol abuse can result in alcoholism. For purposes of diagnosis, the progression of alcoholism is divided into three stages: the early phase, the middle or crucial phase and the chronic or late phase.

The following are the symptoms commonly associated with each phases:

Phase I: Early Phase

- First blackout
- Drinking to relieve stress and anxiety
- Sneaking/hiding
- Loss of memory
- Difficulty to stop even when others do
- Avoidance of discussion of drinking

Phase II: Middle or Crucial Phase

- Loss of control
- Physical and moral deterioration
- Consumption is heavy but not conspicuous
- Start of loosing things
- Alibis and excuses
- Extravagance
- Aggression (verbal and physical)
- Persistent remorse
- Period abstinence
- Change in chemical use pattern
- Loss of friendship
- Loss of position (employment, family, etc)
- First treatment attempt
- Resentment (self/others)
- Escape
- Protecting supply/use
- Morning usage of chemicals

Phase III: Chronic or Late Phase
- More or less continuous use beyond an 18 hr-period
- Ethical deterioration
- Inconsistent inappropriate thinking
- Decrease of tolerance (drinks less to get same effect)
- Indefinable fears
- Tremors (shaking of hand)
- Marked prolonged periods of intoxication
- Serious problems: physical, mental, professional and personal relationships
- Even brief withdrawal from alcohol produces unpleasant and frightening symptoms and the alcoholic drinks to avoid them.
- Tolerance abruptly diminishes—even small amounts cause DRUNKENNESS!

The progression of alcohol carries with it both physical and psychological symptoms. What is noticeable is that as it progresses, the more the behavior becomes out of control and secretive. Feelings of guilt and frustration are also part of the mix. Like any disease, an intervention on earlier stages increases positive prognosis.

What ever happened to Valerie...

The grace of God entered my life when I was 28. My name is Valerie and I'm a grateful recovering alcoholic. I met someone who was four months sober. I was extremely in awe of him, that someone could go four whole months without a drink. He took me to my first AA meeting and I felt something I hadn't felt in years. I felt hope. I saw people with genuine peace of mine – although I confess, at first I didn't really believe people who claimed they had gone years without drinking.

I had the gift of desperation and went from meeting to meeting until I found several I was comfortable at. I changed groups and sponsors when I needed to, but from that day on, I didn't drink. I'm not going to pretend it was easy. I had days in my first year when I wanted to drink so bad I lay in bed in the fetal position rocking saying "Please help me not to drink just for today just for today just for today." In fact the concept of not drinking for one day sounded so enormous to me at first, and I was taught if you can't stop for a day at a time, then stop for one minute at a time. I learned that AA is not a religious program, it's a spiritual program and there's a huge difference. You have to go to a whole lot of meetings to really understand that statement.

I haven't found it necessary to pick up a drink for 20 years. In the 12 steps of recovery, I have learned the freedom to choose a God of my understanding. I have learned about self-respect.

I have no doubt that without AA, I would be dead by now. A friend of mine has a cousin who died of cirrhosis of the liver at 45 years old. The very fact that I am alive is a gift that without AA I wouldn't have received. I am truly grateful...

—Valerie X

TWENTY QUESTIONS — Could I be an Alcoholic?

Are you an alcoholic? To answer this, ask yourself the following questions and answer them as honestly as you can:

1. Do you lose time from school or work due to drinking?
2. Is drinking making your home life unhappy?
3. Do you drink because you are shy with other people?
4. Do you drink to build up your self-confidence?
5. Is drinking affecting your reputation?
6. Have you ever felt remorse after drinking?
7. Have you gotten into financial or legal difficulties as a result of drinking?
8. Do you turn to lower companions and an inferior environment when drinking?
9. Does your drinking make you careless of your friends or family's welfare?
10. Has your ambition decreased since drinking?
11. Have you ever been arrested for or received a driving under the influence citation one or more times as a result of your drinking?
12. Have you ever been involved in an automobile accident as a direct result of your drinking?
13. Does drinking cause you to have difficulty in sleeping?
14. Has your efficiency decreased since drinking?
15. Is drinking jeopardizing your school or job performance?
16. Do you drink to escape from worries or trouble?
18. Do you drink alone?
19. Have you ever had a complete loss of memory as a result of drinking?
20. Has your physician ever treated you for drinking?

If you see yourself in this chapter see your school guidance counselor for help or utilize the resources provided in this book for help. If out of control drinking applies to a friend, or a family member there are resources in the back of this book to get help for friends and families of alcoholics. Usually the problem drinker or alcoholic is the last to know they need help and recovery may start with you.

Chapter Four
Hidden Scars-Lives Lost to
Drug Addiction

He was a tri-athlete, a good student, played hockey, baseball, ran road races, had girlfriends, enjoyed life, was planning on going to college—and Nick Saba, the outgoing and affable teenager, never hurt any body. Until addiction overtook him. "Little did I know that one OxyContin pill at a prom party my sophomore year would alter my life. He used OxyContin for one year before moving on to Heroin. I went from star hockey player to living in the streets, to ending up in jail. I threw my whole life away. I didn't see it coming. It happened so fast. I become a fiend," said Saba. "It absolutely crushed me. I wasn't even a person. I felt crushed like I didn't even exist, and I didn't care about it. This is what this drug did to me"

Nick's story is one of sickness and struggle, of immeasurable loss and incremental gain. He was an athlete who rose to stardom at Tauton's Coyle-Cassidy High School before falling into the netherworld of narcotics. His was a home teeming with life, bursting with promise that, in just a matter of months, teetered on the brink of tragedy.

Nick says the grip of addiction had him thinking "about killing myself many, many times. I wanted to grab a rope and end it. I thought about OD'ing on purpose, and came close a few times" Craig Murray-The Enterprise

Copyright 2007 the Enterprise Gatehouse Medica Inc.

If anyone would have told me that either one of my adorable precocious little boys (one blond and one dark haired) would suffer some of the severe consequences of drug or alcohol addiction when they were younger I would not have believed it. As you read in my first chapter I have seen the ravages of drug addiction in my own life. To say that I have a personal stake in sharing the hell I have endured to save someone else this addictive fate is an understatement.

If you thumb throughout this book still thinking you are smarter than the person that is addicted...you can stop anytime you want... *addiction could never happen to you...think again.* Many addicts can tell you they started out innocently by trying an *OxyContin* or ecstasy pill given to them by a friend at a party and the next thing they know they have dropped out of college are stealing, or prostituting them- selves to support their habit and they are on the street...if they are still lucky to be alive.

The effects of drug addiction are felt on many levels: personal, friends and family, and societal. Individuals who use drugs and alco- hol experience a wide array of physical effects due to their drug and alcohol addiction that they had never anticipated. One such example is the depression an individual feels following their use of cocaine. Additional effects of drug addiction include tolerance, withdrawal, sickness, overdose, and resorting to a life of crime.

Family and friends feel the effects of drug addiction as well. The user's preoccupation with the substance, plus its effects on mood and performance, can lead to relationship problems, poor school and work performance or dismissal. The effects of drug addiction can disrupt family life and create destructive patterns of codependency, that is, friends or whole families, out of love or fear of consequences, inadvertently enables the user to continue using drugs by covering up, supplying money, or denying there is a problem.

Commonly Abused Drugs and How they Are Used

Drugs are administered to or enter the human body in a number of ways, including injection, inhalation, and ingestion. The method of administration impacts on how the drug affects the person. For example: injection takes the drug directly into the blood stream, providing more immediate effects; while ingestion requires the drug to pass through the digestive system, delaying the effects.

Factors Affecting Absorption/Metabolism

Factors that affect absorption/metabolism include physical, emotional and drug-related factors.

Physical Factors

Physical factors that affect the absorption or metabolism of a drug include:

> Person's weight and age – The amount of physical mass a drug must travel through will have an outcome of the drug's total effect on the body. Also, the aging process affects the manner in which the drug exerts its effects on the body.

> Individual biomedical/chemical make-up – Each individual tolerates substances differently. For example: a person's physical condition as well as hypersensitivity (allergies) or hyposensitivity (need for larger doses to gain the desired effect) will influence the total effect of the drug on the individual.

Rate of metabolism – Each drug metabolizes or processes within the body at a different rate. The drug remains active in the body until metabolism occurs. For example: certain medications require dosages to be taken every four, twelve or twenty-four hours, depending on the duration and rate at which the drug is metabolized.

Food – Food in the body slows absorption of the drug into the body by not allowing it to pass directly through the digestive process without first being processed by the digestive system. A slower process occurs, since the body is digesting food in addition to the substance or drug utilized by the person.

Emotional Factors

Factors that may influence drug absorption and metabolism within the body are:

Emotional state – A person's specific emotional state or degree of psychological comfort or discomfort will influence how a drug may affect the individual. For example: if a person began using alcohol and was extremely angry or upset, the alcohol could intensify this anger or psychological discomfort. On the other hand, if alcohol was being used as part of celebration, the psychological state of pleasure could be enhanced by the use of the drug.

Anticipation/Expectancy – The degree, to which a person believes that a given drug will affect them, may have an effect on their emotional state. If a person truly believes that by using a substance, they will experience a given effect, then their expectations may cause a psychological change in the manner in which the drug affects them.

Drug-Related Factors

The drug-related factors that influence the way drugs are absorbed and metabolized within the body are:

Tolerance – Tolerance refers to the amount of a given substance necessary to receive its desired effect.

Presence or use of other drugs – The presence or use of other drugs such as prescription, over-the-counter, nicotine, and caffeine also influence the rate of absorption and metabolism of drugs in the body.

Method of administration - A drug injected directly into the blood stream will affect an individual at a greater rate, since it will be directly absorbed through the blood stream and presented to various organs. If a drug is snorted or inhaled, the effects may be enhanced, due to the fact that the sinus cavity is located in close proximity to the brain. On the other hand, if a drug is ingested, the effects may be slower due to the fact that they must pass through the digestive system.

Physical dependence (addiction) – If a person is physically addicted to a drug, then more of a given substance may be necessary and the effects on the body will differ from those seen in a non-dependent individual.

Elimination

Drugs are eliminated from the body primarily through the liver. The liver and kidneys act as a body's filter to filter out and excrete drugs from the body. The liver metabolizes ninety percent of alcohol in the body, while ten percent is excreted through the lungs and sweat. Also, the liver metabolizes drugs in a fairly consistent manner. For example: alcohol is removed at the rate of one 12 oz. can of beer, one 5 oz. glass of wine or 1 $\frac{1}{2}$ oz. shot of whiskey per hour.

Short-term and long-term effects of Drugs

Marijuana: Pot, Bud, Bomb, Tree or The Kind

Absorption
- Marijuana may be inhaled or ingested.

Short-term Effects
- Increases in heart rate, body temperature, and appetite
- Drowsiness
- Dryness of the mouth and throat
- Reddening of the eyes and reduction in ocular pressure

Long-term Effects
- Can cause the following medical conditions: respiratory problems, lung damage, and cancer
- Memory and concentration impairments
- Possible motivational syndrome

Cocaine: Blow, Big C, Nose Candy, The Lady in White, Rock and Snow.

One of the most dangerous drugs on college campuses is cocaine. According to the 2006 survey on drug use and health, over 35 million Americans age 12 and older have tried cocaine at least once. It is estimated that there are around 2 million cocaine addicts in the United States. Adults 18-25 currently have the highest percentage of cocaine users than any other group. Approximately 7.7% of college students surveyed in 2006 reported lifetime use of cocaine.

Cocaine is a drug extracted from the leaves of the coca plant, and has been around for more than 100 years. It is a brain stimulant and a powerfully addictive drug. On the streets it can be obtained in two forms. The first is a white crystalline powder which can be snorted or dissolved in water and injected. The other is **crack cocaine**, which is a rock-like substance (freebase or rock cocaine) created by processing with ammonia or baking soda. **Crack cocaine** can be smoked and is much more fast-acting than powdered cocaine. The faster the absorption, the more intense the high.

No matter how it is ingested, cocaine use results in quick absorption and instantaneous euphoria. During this brief period of euphoria, the user experiences energy, heightened senses, alertness and mental clarity. It can temporarily decrease the need for food or sleep. These are all appealing sensations for the average college student, who may be overwhelmed with academic requirements.

But the brief euphoria passes quickly, in anywhere from five to thirty minutes, leaving the user hungry for more. They experience a "coke crash" and are irritable and fatigued. Frequently the user is compelled to chase for more and more of this experience. They may sell their possessions or steal the possessions of others to meet this compulsion. They are compelled to experience the euphoria again at any price. This is the nature of addiction.

Cocaine is a dangerous drug and you can't predict which dose is the dose that will leave you physically dependent on it (addicted) or which is the dose that will kill you. One of the things that makes it dangerous is dealers often mix it with other substances. This may be done with items such as sugar or cornstarch to make a supply of cocaine stretch further and to make the user want to come back for more. It may also be mixed with amphetamines.

Cocaine is sometimes glamorized in the movies, but there is nothing glamorous about a substance that would make you steal from family and friends, neglect your health and appearance and possibly experience sudden death. Sudden death has been known to occur even in first-time users.

Absorption
- Cocaine enters the body in one of three ways: injection, smoking or snorting.

Metabolism/Elimination
- Cocaine is a strong stimulant to the central nervous system. Its effects can last anywhere from 20 minutes to several hours, depending on the content, purity, administration, and dosage of the drug.

- Cocaine is responsible for the most drug-related emergency room visits. The use of this substance can result in very serious side-effects, even if used only short term. These side effects include:

Short-term Effects

- Anxiety
- Restlessness
- Chest pains
- Heart attacks
- Cardiac arrest
- Respiratory arrest
- Stroke
- Seizures
- Headaches
- Abdominal pain and nausea
- Coordination problems

Long-term Effects

- May cause extreme alertness, watchfulness, impaired judgment, impulsiveness, and compulsively repeated acts
- May cause stuffiness, runny nose, tissue deterioration inside the nose, and perforation of the nasal septum

Heroin: Big H, Smack, Hell Dust

A-bomb: Marijuana mixed with heroin

Dragon rock: Heroin mixed with cocaine

Nose drops: Liquefied heroin

Speedball: Heroin and cocaine

What Heroin does:

- Gives the user a surge of euphoria or "rush"
- Creates a feeling of warmth on skin a dry mouth and heavy extremities

- After the rush, users go" on the nod," an alternately wakeful and drowsy state
- Clouds mental function
- Depresses respiration
- Can cause collapsed veins, infection of the heart lining and valves, abscesses, and liver disease over prolonged use.

Signs of Heroin Addiction

- Missing spoons, or burn marks on the bottom of spoons
- Belts with teeth marks on them
- Powder on coins
- Itching
- Sweating
- Pinned Pupils
- Weight loss
- Dark eye circles
- Track, or needle marks
- Discarded cigarette filters

When you stop using Heroin

- Withdrawal symptoms can appear in a few hours
- An addict can suffer from vomiting, insomnia, muscle and bone pain, restlessness, diarrhea, and cold flashes
- Symptoms can subside after a week
- People in poor health can die
- Major symptoms peak between 48 and 72 hours after the last dose

Opiates: Oxycontin, Percocet, Perodan, Morphine, Demerol, Davon, Darvocet and Codeine, Opium Heroin

Absorption
- Opiates are normally absorbed through injection

Metabolism/Elimination
- Opiates are metabolized by the liver and may have a lengthy metabolism due to excessive half-lives of the drugs

Short-term Effects
- Include drowsiness, dizziness, mental confusion, constriction of pupils, and euphoria
- Some opiate drugs, such as codeine, demerol, and darvon, also have stimulating effects
- Stimulating effects include: central nervous system excitation, increased blood, elevated blood pressure, increased heart rate, tremors, and seizures

Long-term Effects
- May include impaired vision, pulmonary complications, and menstrual irregularity
- A person may experience nightmares, hallucinations, and mood swings

CRYSTAL METH: Crank, Ice, Crystal, Glass, Chalk
Colleges have a hidden drug epidemic which involves its own home-grown version of one drug. It is called methamphetamine. Whatever you call it, meth is on a silent march to destroy lives. According to www.msnbc.com (http://www.msnbc.msn.com/id/3071772/), more than a million Americans used meth in 1999, more than used crack or heroin.

Its appeal is extreme energy, which puts college students at particular risk. Keeping up with requirements is a challenge for many college students, and the pursuit of wakefulness can lead students down the road of no return. Substance abuse is a way to trick the body into doing what needs to be done. But with crystal meth, 9 out of 10 people who inject it just once become addicted. It is one of the most difficult addictions to beat.

This is not a new drug, but an old drug in new form. Methamphetamine is a super-charged version of amphetamine, which is a prescription drug. Amphetamine was first marketed in the 1930's under the name benzedrine as an inhaler to treat nasal congestion. It was eventually marketed in pill form to treat narcolepsy and attention deficit hyperactivity disorder (ADHD). As time went on, amphetamine abuse became more and more frequent. Amphetamines began being used as a cure-all for people who needed to stay awake. It was also used for weight loss, for helping athletes perform better and longer and for treating mild depression. By 1965, the FDA implemented tighter controls on amphetamines in an effort to control abuse. Many amphetamine products were removed from the market.

Controls placed on amphetamines resulted in a dramatic growth in production of methamphetamines. Methamphetamine comes in clear crystal or powder and dissolves easily in water or alcohol. It can be taken orally, injected, snorted or smoked.

crystal meth is the synthetic white crystalline powder form of amphetamines. It is typically manufactured in illegal labs using readily available materials such as battery acid, antifreeze and drain cleaner. The fact that it is so easy and inexpensive to make using common materials adds to its appeal. Meth labs are found in trailer parks, apartment buildings, motel rooms, abandoned cars and campgrounds. A lasting high is achieved with small quantities and it has been called "the poor man's cocaine."

In low doses, it heightens the senses and makes users more alert. Users quickly reach a level of tolerance with this drug, and require more and more for the same effect. As doses increase, so does exhilaration and euphoria. But high doses also lead to increased heart rate. Body temperature may rise to dangerous levels. Users may have seizures or accumulate fluid in their lungs, brain tissue and skull. Smoking and inhaling meth damages the lungs and nasal passages; injecting the drug puts the user at risk for HIV or Hepatitis C.

How can you tell if someone is using meth?

Signs of meth use are similar to other drugs which stimulate the central nervous system. They include the following:

- Inability to sleep, often for days on end
- Extremely alert and energized, even after being up all night
- Decreased appetite, may become dangerously thin
- Irritability, extreme nervousness, tremors
- Lack of interest in maintaining personal appearance
- Loss of interest in school or extracurricular activities
- Wild mood swings, hostility, paranoia
- Hallucinations or delusions, particularly of insects under the skin leading to excessive scratching
- Burns, nosebleeds or track marks
- Evidence of inhaling or injecting paraphernalia such as straws, spoons, razor blades, mirrors, syringes or surgical tubing

Amphetamines

Absorption
- Amphetamines are absorbed by the body in one of three ways: snorting, swallowing, or injection.

Metabolism/Elimination
- Amphetamines are eliminated through the liver.

Short-term Effects
- A person may experience a loss of appetite, increased alertness, and a feeling of well-being.
- A person's physical condition may be altered by an increase in breathing and heart rate, elevation in blood pressure, and dilation of pupils.

Long-term Effects
- Anxiety and agitation
- Sleeplessness
- Higher blood pressure and irregular heart beat
- Increased susceptibility

If you are having a problem with meth, or any drugs seek help immediately. The dangers of this drug can't be overemphasized. Increased heart rate can lead to heart attack, liver or kidney failure or stroke. If you think this drug won't destroy your life, think again. To see the toll meth takes, visit

http://www.drugfree.org/Portal/DrugIssue/MethResources/faces/index.html

to see the faces of meth. For real stories about the impact meth has had on people, visit

http://www.drugfree.org/Portal/DrugIssue/Meth/stories.html.

My son Chris's story....

The Dark Side of Crystal Meth...

I had my first drink of beer when I was 7, I saw my father with a can of Budweiser and I asked for a sip...My dad said son you won't like it but I insisted, I took a drink and said " eeh that's gross" and my dad said I told you so....

I started smoking pot at 12 when my older brother, Brandon and his friends said they wanted to get me high. I was always doing what I was asked to do wanting to be part of the crowd. I did not think of the consequences. I smoked pot for about 2 years and drank a lot of alcohol. I was stealing Vodka from Payless everyday. I was in the experimental stages of my addiction.

When I was 13, I was sent to juvenile hall for stealing but is was my friends that were stealing and I happened to be with them so I was released. I went to juvenile hall again at age 14 for joy riding. When I was 14 one of my friends Danny told me that his dad had gotten him some new stuff and to come over after school to try it. Danny was the same age as myself and his dad was a biker. I followed him home on my bike we went into his army bunker he pulled out this pink beige crystal stuff prop dope (prophynall) stuck it in a light bulb to melt it. This stuff was so powerful the light bulb just desingrated. The dope was dry so we crushed it and sniffed a line I was up for 3 days.

Then I started to use crystal meth about once a week or couple times a month. I was able to function and hide most of my drug use from my parents. I was then in the functional stage of my addiction where I could function, go to school but still I was using drugs.

When my parents got divorced I was 15 I moved to another town with my mom and 16-year-old brother Brandon. My brother and I were in trouble constantly drinking and using drugs the police were at my mom's house weekly.

I was selling crystal meth at 16 to make my own money. I got so out of control that my mom put me in a residential drug rehab the Bill Wilson Center. My parents saw the danger of my drug use and were doing every thing they could to help me get clean and stay clean. My mom had enough and I went to live with my dad for a short time. His wife kicked me out at 16 and I ended up at a boys ranch in Morgan Hill, California.

The first time I went jail was Sept 18 1998 for second degree burglary, evading the police and a DUI. I got my charges dropped to a misdemeanor and did 60 days work furlough.

By the time in was in early 20's I was in the chronic stage of my drug addiction and spent my whole 21st year in prison. When I say chronic stage I mean that my whole life revolved around my addiction, using drugs and getting drugs. I became so twisted in my addiction that even being pulled over by a police officer I did not want to let go of my drugs even knowing the possible consequences. The drugs take control of you and every decision you make.

At one point when I was in the deep of my drug use, living on the streets my mom filed a restraining order against me for about 2 years I could not contact her. If I came to her door she called the police. I have seen my mom cry more times than I can count over her fear of losing me. She would only help me if I was willing to go to rehab nothing more. I did go to rehab several times but I still struggled with relapse.

I have been to prison 4 times, San Quentin, Tracy State prison, Susanville, Delano, Chino and Avenal all behind my *drug use. I am now 28 and I have spent the last seven years in and out of jail in my disease of drug & alcohol addiction. This disease of addiction is cunning, baffling and powerful and can be fatal if not treated. I am fortunate that I am now in recovery, living one day at a time and by the grace of god I am still alive.*

If I have only one thing to say to you it is make your own choices be secure in yourself and do not worry about what other people think about you. Be who you are on your own, you are enough. Don't even experiment with drugs and alcohol it will steal your life away from you as it did with me.

—Chris B…

Sedative Hypnotics: Benzo's Barbiturates, Benzodiazepines)

Benzodiazepines mediate many of the same symptoms as barbiturates, but are far less toxic and have a strongly reduced risk of overdose. This is not to say they are not without their own risks; where barbiturates pose a greater "front-end" danger in that overdose or drug/alcohol interactions may result in fatality, benzodiazepines pose a greater "back-end" risk in the possibility of addiction, dependence, and serious physical and psychological withdrawal symptoms. Immediate cessation of long-term benzodiazepine use instead of tapering can be dangerous and have serious effects.

Absorption
- Sedative hypnotics are absorbed through ingestion

Metabolism/Elimination
- Sedative hypnotics are eliminated by the liver and excreted in urine. Their effect can last anywhere from two to ten hours

Short-term Effects

- Short-term effects can occur with low to moderate use.
- May experience moderate relief of anxiety and a sense of well-being
- There may be temporary memory impairment, confusion, and impaired thinking
- A person could be in a stupor, and have altered perception and slurred speech

Long-term Effects

- May include over-sedation, decreased motivation, apathy, and lack of interest in surroundings
- A person may experience headaches, dizziness, sleep disorders, anxiety, depression, and tremors
- There may be an increase in appetite and impairment of thinking, memory, and judgment

San José State University Prevention Education Program Drug Abuse Screening Test

Please answer the following questions with yes or no

1. Have you used drugs other than those required for medical reasons?

2. Have you abused prescription drugs?

3. Do you abuse more than one drug at a time?

4. Can you get through the week without using drugs (other than those required for medical reasons)?

5. Are you always able to stop using drugs when you want to?

6. Do you abuse drugs on a continuous basis?

7. Do you try to limit your drug use to certain situations?

8. Have you had "blackouts" or "flashbacks" as a result of drug use?

9. Do you ever feel bad about your drug abuse?

10. Does your significant other (or parents) ever complain about your involvement with drugs?

11. Do your friends or relatives know or suspect you abuse drugs?

12. Has drug abuse ever created problems between you and your significant other?

13. Has any family member ever sought help for problems related to drug use?

14. Have you ever lost friends because of your use of drugs?

15. Have you ever neglected your family or missed work because of your use of drugs?

16. Have you ever been in trouble at work because of drug abuse?

17. Have you ever lost a job because of drug abuse?

18. Have you gotten into fights when under the influence of drugs?

19. Have you ever been arrested because of unusual behavior while under the influence of drugs?

20. Have you ever been arrested for driving while under the influence of drugs?

21. Have you engaged in illegal activities in order to obtain drugs?

22. Have you been arrested for possession of dangerous drugs?

23. Have you ever experienced withdrawal symptoms as a result of heavy drug intake?

24. Have you had medical problems as a result of your drug use (e.g., memory loss, hepatitis, convulsions, bleeding, etc.)?

25. Have you ever gone to anyone for help for a drug problem?

26. Have you ever been in a hospital for medical problems related to drug use?

27. Have you ever been involved in a treatment program specifically related to drug care?

28. Have you been treated as an outpatient for problems related to drug use?

29. If you think you have an addiction to drugs run don't walk to get help your life may depend on it.

For further information visit the resources in the back of this book and the following sites:

Office of National Drug Control Policy at
http://www.whitehousedrugpolicy.gov/drugfact/index.html

The Partnership for a Drug-Free America at
http://www.drugfree.org/

Narcotics Anonymous at http://www.na.org.

"Life is the sum of all our choices."
—Albert Camus

Chapter 5
Don't Bet On It—Campus Gambling

Gambling is the nations' foremost "silent addiction." As one college counselor pointed out, *pathological gamblers* don't have track marks on their arms, their speech isn't slurred and they are not staggering down the street. But on the inside, the emotional churn going on is equally as great (as a substance abuser)" (as quoted in Henry, 2003) The results can be devastating, as pathological gamblers find themselves unable to keep up with rent or tuition, maxing out their credit cards or overdrawing bank accounts, lying, turning to theft, dealing drugs or prostitution, getting arrested, or in some cases even suicide (Wexler & Iesnber, 2002)

> **In one extreme case, a student at the University of Wisconsin murdered three roommates because he owed them thousands in gambling debts. The trio had helped him place bets with an off-shore gambling company. He had lost $15,000 through gambling and withdrawn $72,000 from his bank account to support his habit before he committed the murders.**

Compared to drugs and alcohol, which have been around the college scene for ages, the addiction of gambling is a relatively young addiction in campuses. It is, however, one of the most widespread and most serious concerns affecting students today. A gambling network in a school can very easily be disguised as just a group of students getting together. In this internet age, bets can even be made online or via cell phones. It is an addiction that can involve an entire school and yet still be right under everyone's noses. Because the rewards are something that resonates with almost all—money—it seems very harmless and it is very tempting to make fast money.

According to the Annenberg Public Policy Center's 2005 National Center of Youth, there are 2.9 Million Americans ages 14 to 22 who gamble on cards once a week. About 50.4% of male college students and 26.6% of female college students gamble on cards at least once a month—a staggering number. That is half of the entire male student body and a quarter of the female student body!

Gambling is particularly tempting to college students because this is the age when risk-taking behaviors are common. The legal age for gambling is 18 years old in many states, making it therefore a socially permissible behavior. The forms of gambling among students vary greatly depending on the individual student and the school being surveyed. Among the common gambling activities for college students are: casino activities (cards, gambling machines, and playing the lottery), informal games such as playing cards with friends for money, and internet gambling (particularly in poker tournaments). The internet has provided unprecedented access to on-line gambling. Currently, there are over 2,000 gambling websites that take in over $4 billion annually (Aire, 2003)

Gambling for the compulsive gambler is defined as follows: Any betting or wagering for self or others, whether for money or not, no matter how slight or insignificant, where the outcome is uncertain or depends upon chance or "skill" constitutes gambling—Gamblers Anonymous

It's 2 am I've got an economics exam very early in the morning. I can stay on for just one more tournament. This time I can win I can feel it. I need to make up for what I lost today. I absolutely have too. Maybe I could buy a new outfit for this

weekend or put a little bit of money towards my credit card bill. I can feel it. This is the one. Come on. Aces, aces...I am an addict. I'm not alone. There is a new addiction plaguing college campuses online gambling. My 2 a.m. pre-econ exam late-night binge is what I call the "gambling me". The reason I didn't connect it directly to myself is due to the fact that I never knew I was capable of an addiction. I've never smoked or done drugs and only drink socially. I was the last person in the entire world what I thought could be addicted to anything...
—Lauren Patrizi, Loyola University—2005

Sports Betting

Sports wagering, beginning in high school and increasing in college is done by 50% of student-athletes (Engwall, Hunter, & Steinberg, 2003). Lesieur (1991) reported 85% of college athletes as having participated in betting and 23% surveyed showed evidence of pathological gambling behavior.

Being physically and psychologically tied to a campus, college students are more interested in the outcomes of sporting events, and when combined with easy access to alcohol and high seed internet, many postsecondary institutions find their student engaging at much higher rates than the general population (Henry,2003 Sperber 2000)

According to the University of Kansas Director of Counseling Services, gambling allows students to feel intimately involved in a game (Aire, 2000) Another gambling recovery counselor stated, "The more someone knows about a given sport, the more they may believe their decision-making give them a significant advantage. This develops a level of emotional invincibility in the addiction" (as quoted in Henry 2003). With easy access to gambling and a need to feel a part of the larger organization, pathological gambling associated with betting on sporting events has risen significantly in the past ten years. (Serber 2000)

The only thing I was studying in college was the football lines...

My gambling, drinking and use of drugs started my fresh-man year at Santa Clara University where I was enrolled on a baseball scholarship. I was introduced to the campus bookie who played baseball with me! He took all kinds of bets from horse racing to football. At first I bet small amounts on NFL games and immediately went on a winning streak, which as it turned out was the seal of doom for me! It seemed too easy and it definitely was an ego booster to have other students ask me who I was betting on that week! I started out betting $20 to $40 at a time but after I began winning, my wagers went up to $200.00 to $400.00 a game. I had parlayed my winnings to over $3000.000, which back in the late 70's was a lot to a guy working part-time waiting tables. My job, my studies, my social life was all negatively affected by my gambling.

I quit my job believing I had found my way to make money. I would be late or miss classes from staying up late celebrat-ing my good fortune. The only thing I was studying were the football lines. When my friends were out doing fun things, I would be with my gambling buddies partying with alcohol, pot, and cocaine! I found the new loves of my life gambling and partying! I put playing baseball and my studies on the back burner! Even women took a back seat to my newfound addictions! I wasn't interested in anything but feeling the adrenaline rush I felt from gambling being "in action" and partying, which began to compliment each other quite nicely. I continued this lifestyle through my freshman year. My grades of course suffered and so did my performance on the baseball field.

My sophomore year in college I met my first wife and was still partying and using drugs. Even though she partied with me she did not know that I was carrying on my secret life of gambling down a very dark and destructive path. Hiding my secret addiction and a lack of explanation of where the money was going was the demise of our marriage...(more on Frankie later in this book)

There are several reasons why on-line gambling particularly on college sports, is popular among college students. No tangible, cash money is involved, lending an air of detachment to actual losses or making it difficult for gambler to keep track of their losses. In fact 95% of on-line gambling is done with credit card (Aire 2003). On-line gambling is accessible, particularly on college campuses where computers with high-speed internet access are prevalent and available 24 hours a day.

My worst gamble in life was getting a bookie...

As with most people who have addictions, my gambling started very innocently. I was introduced to sports parlay cards by a high school friend around age 20. Growing up in El Paso, Texas, it was a short drive over to Mexico where gambling was legal for those over 18 (although I never once saw anyone ask for identification at the wagering window, and a lot of people seemed younger than me.) I would pick out about 5 or 6 NFL games for Sunday as parlay action (meaning all teams must win but you could win 20 times the amount) in the hopes that I could turn a $5 wager into a lot of money. At first it was a way to talk with friends about our picks, go over placing the wagers, maybe go to a bar, and then watch the games together on Sunday. I would consistently pick about 4 or 5 games correctly, but would always be one or two short. This only made me more determined. Over a period of time, I became less interested in the fellowship of friends I had known for several years (some from childhood), and more concerned about the outcome of the games. I knew that I was almost there but was doing something wrong. Then it came to me: I should only bet on one game. The one game I knew for sure would win and just disregard the other games. So one day, I picked out an NBA game I was positive was a "sure thing" and took all my wages from one week of waiting tables ($220) and drove over with eager anticipation. That entire day at school I was obsessed with the outcome of the game, even though I had not even placed the bet yet. I remember placing the bet, driving straight home to my parent's house, and watching the game on TV without eating or taking a bathroom break. The team was a 6-point underdog and won the game by 20 points. I was obviously ecstatic and remember distinctly thinking, "Why should I work when I can spend a little bit of time researching games and then just make money that way." From there, my gambling "career" began.

I soon found myself gambling on nearly a daily basis, even on games that I wasn't sure on, but thought I would win those anyway. I managed to finish x-ray school, get a full-time job at a hospital, date, play sports, hang out with friends, and live on my own. All the while, the amount of time and the amount of wagering increased gradually over time. Soon I found myself becoming "one of those people." You know those people who lack self-discipline, common sense, and will power to stop gambling when things have "gone too far." I always prided myself on hard work and intelligence in all aspects of my life and that I would never stray into a side of life of addicts, dere-licts, and all out general "losers". Yet there I was, maxing out credit cards, living paycheck to paycheck, and working so much overtime just to feed my "habit" of gambling. I found myself becoming alienated from my friends, visiting family less and less, and either failing in relationships with women or staying "stuck" in miserable ones.

My worst gamble in life was getting a bookie. Here was the opportunity to place wagers over the phone, any amount, as many games as I wanted and didn't have to front the money. I started out on a hot streak and soon found myself gambling either $500 or $1000 per game. On good weeks I would pick up an envelope filled with money at the local golf shop and on the bad weeks I would find myself using credit cards for cash advances and juggling accounts to scrape together enough money to pay my debts. One bookie would take it easy on me if I was short and wouldn't take any more bets until I settled up and the other one would threaten me to come up with money and then the next week buy me a bottle of alcohol to go with my winnings. This all came to a quick end one year after I moved to Las Vegas when law enforcement approached me about my use of bookmaking services. I had two choices: cooperate and help bring down the bookmaker or go to jail. The choice was simple and after nearly 9 months of taped phone calls and payout done under surveillance my job was done and I was no longer in trouble with the law. Despite a compassionate plea from a concerned agent about my gambling, it continued afterward for 2 more years, despite bankruptcy, trouble at work, and a treatment program and sporadic attendance in Gambler's Anonymous. I tried every imaginable way to gamble like a normal person or stop all together including several moves to different cities, I stopped drinking, working out every day, and various relationships with women. I just couldn't find a way and it made me feel worse every time I gambled knowing that it started out as a just a harmless, fun game.

I have been gambling free for a while now and my life is so much better. For me, I did not fully admit I had a gambling problem until it affected my personal life to a point of unmanageability. It wasn't lack of money, work, broken relationships, anger, deteriorating health, or a pessimistic outlook on life, but a combination of all these things and more. Gambling may be a fun, entertaining way for a majority of people, but when you get the rush of winning a hand of poker, a wager on a baseball game, or scratching a lottery ticket that feels better than anything else in the world, it is hard to ignore and just walk or control that euphoria. Your body and mind craves it like an alcoholic who wants a beer or an addict who wants a hit. This can happen to anyone, no matter how young or old, rich or poor, male or female, black or white you are. In my recovery, I have encountered people from so many walks of life whose lives were destroyed by gambling. The good news is that there is help out there, and you are definitely not alone. Just be honest with yourself, others who care for you, and know that there is no shame in admitting you have a problem. Remember, a smart person learns from his mistakes, but a genius learns from other people's mistakes. Be a genius and learn from people who have suffered before you.

—Bryon C.

http://www.miph.org/Gambling/links.htm The typical problem gambler was male, a weekly or daily user of alcohol or illicit drugs, and someone with a relatively high disposable income and whom had been raised by a parent with a gambling problem.

According to the American Psychological Association, pathological gambling is characterized by preoccupation with gambling, betting increasing amounts, unsuccessful attempts to stop or reduce gambling, lying to hide gambling and jeopardizing important relationships due to gambling.

Phases of Gambling[1]

The progression of gambling is said to have four phases: the winning phase, the losing phase, the desperate phase and the hopeless phase. Taken from www.LostBet.com

The Winning Phase

The start of compulsive gambling is that of immediate gratifi-

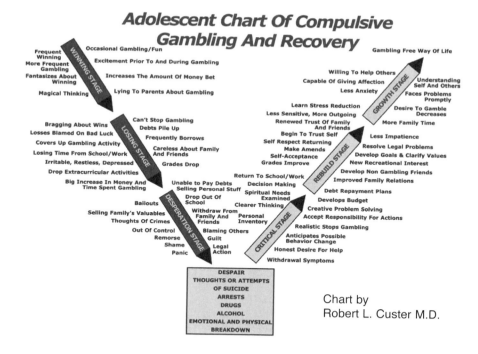

Adolescent Chart Of Compulsive Gambling And Recovery

Chart by
Robert L. Custer M.D.

1 Arizona Council on Compulsive Gambling and the Council on Compulsive Gambling of New Jersey, Inc.

cation—a period where in a gambler likely wins more than he loses. The wins reinforce his love of the sport. During the winning phase, a gambler may develop the illusion that he or she is "skilled" at the game. This phase is usually the first three years of gambling.

The Losing Phase

But the luck does not run forever. After a while he starts losing bets and losing money. Paradoxically, a losing phase does not discourage a gambler. Rather during the losing streak, a gambler feels tempted to gamble more and bet large amounts. He is convinced that he is simply on a losing streak and merely needs that one win to get back his groove. He invests then on "longshots" which, while has low odds of winning, pays big.

He may also engage in a behavior called "chasing losses." This means increasing gambling and bets in the hope to win back the losses. In the period of chasing losses, the lying begins. A gambler would lie in order to maintain the façade that he is winning, still financially viable and competent at his game. He continues to boast about his skills at gambling; talks often about his wins, rarely about his losses. When he suffers his first major "set-back" which places him in a deep financial trouble, he can make up a lie to get a loan. He considers that "bail-out" as a win. He is back in action and gambling even more feverishly than before. These bailouts may occur numerous times; eventually, it is almost impossible to persuade others to again provide a loan. He seems to lose almost all the time now. His life has become unmanageable, and his family life is rapidly deteriorating.

The Desperation Phase

This is the point when the gambler becomes obsessed with gambling already and feels compelled to carry it through. Even knowing that he will lose, he will still carry on with his game. His lying becomes completely out of control. When others don't believe his lies, he becomes angry with them, blaming others for his problems. He must obtain the money with which to gamble at all costs. They have possibly already left or are on the verge of leaving. Illegal activity may be occurring; the gambler may be embezzling money or stealing it in other ways. He will consider these as loans which will be paid back soon from the big win he believes he will have.

The gambler often has an outward appearance, even at this stage, of being in total control. He is still convinced that everyone believes his lies. He even becomes angry when they don't. Outwardly he blames everyone but himself for the unfortunate circumstances now occurring. Inwardly, the gambler is in severe anguish. He truly loves his family and wants things to be like they used to be. He wants respect and stability, but he has to gamble. He can't tell you why, but he has to gamble.

The Hopeless Phase

Until recently only three phases of pathological gambling have been noted. Many clinicians and experts who treat pathological gamblers now say a fourth phase exists for both action and escape gamblers. Once the gambler has been through the desperation phase, it would seem that everything bad had occurred. However in the hopeless phase, pathological gamblers have "given up". They believe nothing can help, they don't care if they live or die, in fact for many the latter is the preference. They will all consider suicide during this phase. Most will commit actions, which could place them in jail or prison. Clinical depression is a given. In their minds, no one cares, no hope is available. The hopeless phase is the time when the pathological gambler either gets help or ends with suicide or prison.

Principal Errors in Thinking Among Gamblers

Gambling is often reinforced by fallacies in thinking that gamblers use. One way to prevent and control gambling therefore is to evaluate one's thinking and see if they are based on realistic odds. The following are some concepts commonly misunderstood by a compulsive gambler.

Independence of Turns

It is not unusual for gamblers to think in terms of 'streaks.' They might say "I will definitely win today, I am on a winning streak." Or "I will not place a bet on that machine, it's on a losing streak." Thus when they get, say, three wins in a row, they interpret it as a strong likelihood that the next bet would win.

Or sometimes gamblers interpret a succession of losses as one that would result in a win soon. For instance they may say, "Its been even numbers that appear all night. Chances are high, the next roll will be an odd number." They may even justify this thought 'statistically', if they've been getting bad rolls for awhile, chances are the next one would result on a win. It is assuming that each of one's turns would subscribe to the law of averages.

These kinds of thinking violate the principle of the independence of turns. Independence of turns means that events are independent of each other; each bet is considered as unique in itself and as having no links to previous and consequent events. Thus there are no such things as lucky streaks or catching up on previous losses. Each bet has a 50-50 chance of winning.

Independence of turns is an essential condition of games of chance. In order to be unpredictable and to obey the rules of chance, all gambling games are structured in a way that each turn is an independent event and in no way determined by the results of the previous turn. This independence, or absence of a link, necessarily renders useless the observation of results with the goal of predicting the next result. Thus, gamblers can never exert any control over the game.

Illusions of Control

The majority of gamblers believe that they accumulate experience and learn from their errors when gambling. In truth, this feeling of personal efficacy is a considerable handicap and gamblers who believe that their actions influence their chances of winning are victims: they maintain the illusion that they will beat the industry by defying the negative winning expectancy by recuperating their losses.

As gambling activities are not games of skill, no mental or physical skills are necessary when it comes to betting. However majority of gamblers believe that it is possible for them to acquire some form of mastery.

Familiarity is an important factor in the illusion of control. The more an individual familiarizes himself with a task determined by chance, the more he has the impression of being able to control the situation. The amount of direct exposure to a situation increases the degree of perceived control.

A number of studies demonstrated that when individuals have the opportunity to discuss the degree of risk that they take, they will take greater risks when they make their decisions alone. Wallach et. al. explained this increase in risk taking as a group process in which the individuals share responsibility and therefore each group member feels less individually responsible for the risk-taking behavior. As a result of the group discussion, an individual becomes more familiar with the situation and this increases a tolerance with risk-taking.

Superstitions

Another common error in thinking among gamblers is the belief in superstitions. Often superstitions support a gamblers illusion of control by making him think that a ritual can increase his chances of a win. Superstitious must also be studies vis-à-vis realistic odds.

Arnie and Sheila Wexler certified compulsive gambling counselors offers the following questions to anyone who may have a gambling problem. These questions are provided to help the individual decide if he or she is a compulsive gambler and wants to stop gambling.

TWENTY-THREE QUESTIONS
Do You Have a Gambling Problem?

Twenty Three Questions- Do you have a gambling problem.

1. Do you find yourself gambling more frequently than you used to?

2. Has anyone ever suggested that you have a problem with gambling?

3. Did you ever gamble more than you intended to? (time or money)

4. Do you have a fantasy that gambling is going to make you rich?

5. Do you believe you have superior knowledge when you place a bet?

6. Do you lose time from school due to gambling?

7. Do you have intense interest in point spreads or odds?

8. Do you make frequent calls to sports phones or lotteries?

9. Have you ever bet with a bookmaker or used credit cards to gamble?

10. Have your grades dropped because of gambling?

11. Have you ever done anything illegal to finance your gambling?

12. Is gambling language or references part of your vocabulary?

13. Do you prefer to socialize with friends who gamble?

14. Does anyone in your family have an addiction?

15. Have you ever borrowed money to finance gambling?

16. Has anyone ever paid your gambling debts for you?

17. Does gambling give you a "rush or high "?

18. Do you find yourself craving another gambling experience?

19. Do you find yourself "chasing: your losses?

20. Have you ever tried to stop or control your gambling?

21. Have you lied about your gambling to family and/or friends?

22. Are you spending more time on the internet?

23. Are you playing poker on the internet?

Most compulsive gamblers will answer yes to at least seven of these questions.

These questions were prepared by:
Arnie and Sheila Wexler Associates
Certified Compulsive Gambling counselors
For more information see the resource guide.

Chapter 6
Feeding the Hungry Heart—
Eating Disorders

The most sincere love of all is the love of food.
—George Bernard Shaw

"I Am Fed Up"

Even before I was to start College I still felt treated like a child. It was so bad that I would have crying spells in my bathroom or in any place where I could be alone. After my mother had a break down I was slowly starting to hating her—except I felt guilty for being such a pain for her. It was a strange combination or emotions—I had so much anger at her and at the same time I wanted her to be happy. I was bursting inside with no one to discuss these things. I did know anyone I thought could understand.

I made new friends at the university—one friend in particular, named Jake. He was a classmate who eventually became my boyfriend. He listened to all the things that I had been keeping inside and had never shared with anyone. For the first time in my life I felt loved for who I was, he accepted me unconditionally.

One night, he found me in my bathroom in the middle of my "purging session". He became understandably upset with me. While I had friends who were suspicious of my bulimia before, I could always convince them that nothing was wrong. Jake and I spent a great deal of time together and he eventually got curious where I would go after every meal. But Jake was different and he was a tough guy to manipulate.

He did not leave me as I thought he would. Rather, he dragged me to the counselor's office the very next day. Actually, he blackmailed me into seeking counseling: its either I talked to the counselor or he would call my mother. Suffice to say, I would rather die than have my mom know. I went with him to the guidance center the next day and it was the best decision that I made.

The school counselor opened my mind to see so many things that had been going on inside me. I was able to release all the anger I felt and the guilt I was trying to manage. Moreover, my counselor encouraged me to seek medical attention for my issues with bulimia. It was hard at first but I managed to stop my self-defeating behavior. Jake was my anchor through all of this. He never showed me once that I disgusted him but he never let me get away with my excuses either. He encouraged me to seek recovery. In some ways I felt like I had found something that I wanted for a long time. Jake became someone who would hold me accountable with patience, as a parent would, which I never had.

You see, my mother was a very controlling woman. I have no doubt that she genuinely loved us three girls. I can say that we loved her very much also. When our father walked out on us to be with another woman she raised my sisters and me single-handedly. Her definition of love of love was suffocating. As I was learning in counseling the term for our relationship: we were "enmeshed." It means that we were so close, so stuck together, in each other's lives, that we cannot breathe. That is not the healthy definition of love.

When my siblings and I were already in our teens, my mother controlled the amount of food that she put on our plates. She determined what we ate and how much. You could not refuse what she put on your plate without a fight. She always gave us way too much food and you could not leave the table until your plate was clean to her satisfaction.

My sisters and I were being treated like were in the military with 24/7 observation. It was too much. I was the eldest of three girls, when I was 15 years old, my sisters were 9 and 7. They obeyed the rules without questions as I did when I was their age. I then began what I considered as my childish rebellion. I started by becoming difficult when called for meals.

I would also return all that I couldn't eat back to the serving dish—even if it was cold and disgusting. Sometimes I would take a new plate for myself, get my food, and sit at the table farthest from her. On one occasion I ignored her and proceeded to eat pizza I ordered from take-out.

As expected these episodes of disobedience were met with hostility. We argued at the table, glared at each other and sometimes even had plates thrown to the floor. Pretty soon our shouting matches became legendary. I felt worse for my sisters; they were caught in the crossfire and were confused as to what is going on. But as bad as it sounds, I felt good that I can annoy my mom and get a rise out of her. I felt better too when I got away with eating what I want—it's like winning a huge struggle for independence.

Our fights started initially about food and about me following the rules she sets as the head of the household. But it wasn't long before we both took the fighting personally. She would often say things like "You don't appreciate me, and all I do for you", "I do things for your own good and this is how you repay me", and my personal favorite was that I thought were particularly off-tangent to the issue at hand, "You are lucky I sacrifice for you instead of abandoning you like your father did"and "Just as I feared, you are growing up just like your Dad! Headstrong and stupid. He did not listen to me either and look where it got him."At that time I was too young to appreciate the fact that she was trying to communicate to me her needs and frustrations—that she was a tired soul needing affirmation for her efforts. I also did not realize that she was verbally abusing me.She needed assurance that I would turn out okay.

I did not realize then that she still had issues from how her marriage ended and she was still carrying and taking it out on me. All I saw and heard was her attempt to use guilt to get me into submission. So I hit her back with my own sentiments: "You try to control everything", "You treat me like a child" and "Well, no wonder dad left you. I would leave you too if I could. In fact, I just might."

Things changed however when my mom had a nervous breakdown. We were having our traditional fight during dinner when she just started screaming and hitting her head on the wall. I got scared. I haven't seen her like this. What have I done? I started apologizing to her. I decided to stop being difficult from then on. However the feeling of being suffocated did not go away.

After I had gone to three years of therapy on my own, it was now time to involve my mother before history repeated its self with my sisters. It was then that I got the courage to confess to my mother how I felt and asked her to seek therapy. What encouraged me was the fact that at that time, my two younger sisters are already adolescents in the stage of seeking autonomy. There was the familiar tension in the table already and it looked like history was about to repeat itself. I felt I had to break the cycle. I told my mother that I loved her, that I had an eating disorder and I was not okay—and neither was she. It was a difficult confrontation but it turned out well. My mother and I went to see a therapist that week.

Therapy gave me more insight about what we were doing to each other. My mother shared her childhood, her own parents abandoned her and her siblings too. No one cared for them for about a week before a relative found them. She and her siblings went hungry for days. Despite being the youngest of five and the only girl, it was her and not her elder brothers who found work and managed to find ways to get them food. For her, being able to provide a meal for her family is her responsibility, it's what sets her apart from the parents who had abandoned her and the siblings who were, in her words, "too weak to be resourceful." When she sees us eating therefore, she sees herself taking care of us. She defines it as her "presence." Consequently if she doesn't see us full she feels like she is abandoning us, like her husband did.

With coaching from the therapist, my sisters and I told her what she needed to hear. "Mom, we are okay. You don't have to worry about us anymore. You take good care of us. We know you are here. You can relax now." One by one, the three of us assured her. By the time the last person spoke up, she was sobbing. It was an emotional moment. But it changed everything our family. Now food to us is just that, food. It is not a way to measure love and success. It is not a way to rebel.

—Kristy

One need not look to regulated substances in order to find solace. Food can very easily be a person's drug of choice. And why not? Eating can be one of life's most pleasurable experiences. Food is not just physically nourishing but may be aesthetically pleasing as well— not to mention just, plain delicious.

More so, eating is one of those behaviors that carries with it many possible symbolic representations of needs provided. Feeding is often a symbol of nurturance: in most cultures creating quality meals for other people is a sign of care. When one is ill, isn't care represented by chicken soup? It can also be a metaphor for what you decide to accept in your person and what you reject. Thus the way you control what food you take inside your body may possibly represent how you wish to control what emotions you allow inside of you.

> *"The act of losing weight is supported nearly everywhere in our culture. Women report that they diet 'not to lose weight' but because 'I feel better when I weigh less…."*
> *–Ruth Raymond Thone*

College students are especially prone to eating disorders. Research shows that more than 90 percent of those who have eating disorders are women between the ages of 12 and 25[1]. The main age of onset of an eating disorder is most common in the college-aged years (age 17 for anorexia; 18-20 for bulimia). Up to ten percent of individuals with eating disorders are male, and many of these men suffer from problems with binge-eating.

More so, college students are more prone to dieting-related behaviors that may possibly become a precursor to eating disorders. The Massachusetts Eating Disorders Association estimates that 90% of female college students engage in diet-related behaviors. This is attribute to a felt pressure to subscribe to a particular body image which, as media would have been, is often on the thin and willow side.

1 National Alliance for the Mentally Ill, 2003

College Female Athletes Are At High Risk

Female athletes represent a subgroup of the population at increased risk of developing eating disorders. Athletic competition and demands for performance may lead to perfectionism in many areas, including the body. Athletes who engage in sports that emphasize slenderness or in which lean body weight is a factor in performance (e.g. track, rowing, gymnastics, diving, wrestling, figure-skating, dance, cheerleading) are particularly vulnerable to developing an eating disorder. Often, moderate weight loss in these sports may improve performance which further reinforces unhealthy eating practices. However, eventually athletic performance becomes compromised by the factors of emotional exhaustion, physical fatigue, poor nutrition and medical problems that are part of an eating disorder

This prevalence is particularly alarming as eating disorders are one of the most fatal psychological conditions. The mortality rate for anorexia, for example, is higher than for any other psychological disorder; 1 in 10 anorexics will die from the effects of starvation, including cardiac arrest, or from suicide.

Without treatment, up to twenty percent (20%) of people with serious eating disorders die. With treatment, that number falls to two to three percent (2-3%). In 2005, Dr. Wright of the Eating Disorders Program at Presbyterian Hospital in Dallas, Texas indicated that the mortality rate for untreated anorexia nervosa may be even higher, up to 25 percent.

Do you or someone you know have an Eating Disorder?

Anorexia nervosa

Research suggests that about one percent (1%) of female adolescents have anorexia. That means that about one out of every one hundred young women between ten and twenty are starving themselves, sometimes to death. There do not seem to be reliable figures for younger children and older adults, but such cases, while they do occur, are not common.

Anorexics commonly engage in behavior related to controlling weight, such as counting calories, exercising excessively, avoiding food or picking what they eat. They have an intense fear of gaining weight or becoming fat—even if they are already underweight. In fact, anorexia is conceived as a disease of perception: they have a distorted body image. They often overestimate their body size and cannot realistically appreciate the danger that they are putting themselves in.

Anorexics are often classified as the "restrictive" type or the "binge eating/ purging" type. The former are anorexics who keep their weight down solely by restricting their food intake and are not currently purging or binge eating. The latter kind binge and purge themselves via vomiting or taking laxatives, diuretics or enemas.

This disorder takes its physical toll on the person. Long-term starvation causes muscle weakness and loss of muscle strength, which also affects the heart. Sufferers may develop cardiac abnormalities and arrhythmias. They may have dry skin and excessive growth of dry brittle hair over the nape of the neck, cheeks, forearms and thighs. They often have cold hands and feet and peripheral edema.

Bulimia nervosa

Research suggests that about four percent (4%), or four out of one hundred, college-aged women have bulimia. About 50% of people who have been anorexic develop bulimia or bulimic patterns. Because people with bulimia are secretive, it is difficult to know how many older people are affected. Bulimia is rare in children.

More than ten percent of adolescent girls and three percent of boys binge eat or purge at least once a week, according to a study published in *Archives of Pediatric and Adolescent Medicine.* (June 2008)

Bulimia is an eating disorder characterized by alternate urges of uncontrollable overeating and compensatory behaviors to prevent weight gain like starving themselves or worse vomiting or purging to control weight.

Binge Eating Disorder

The largest group of people with eating disorders is those described as having binge eating disorders. These are the people who experience marked distress about overeating but cannot be diagnosed as having bulimia nervosa.

Binge eating is defined as eating, in a discrete period of time, an amount of food that is larger than most people would eat in a similar period of time under similar circumstances. According to the Diagnostic Manual of Mental Disorders-IV, binge episodes are associated with at least three of the following: eating much more rapidly than normal, eating until feeling uncomfortably full, eating large amounts of food when not feeling physically hungry, eating alone because of embarrassment about amount eaten and feeling disgusted with oneself, depressed or very guilty after over eating.

Comfort Eating AKA Compulsive Overeating

As with most addictions, eating disorders may be understood as a way to medicate an emotional struggle. Compulsive overeating for example has been described as a way to derive 'comfort', a way to fill a large hole and avoid feelings of 'emptiness.'

Geneen Roth, author of the book Feeding the Hungry Heart, speaks of binges this way: *"Binges are purposeful acts, not demented journeys. They do not signify a lack of willpower or the inability to care for yourself. On the contrary, a binge can actually be an urgent attempt to care for yourself when you feel uncared for."*

There are often times when you are lonely, or when you've experienced something that makes you think less of your self that you find solace in emotional eating. Food after all is reliable. They always make you feel taken care of without demanding anything in return.

Here are a series of questions that may help you determine if you have an unhealthy relationship with food.

The Feelings Behind The Fork

Feelings

Are you a perfectionist, a person who always wants to be in control, an overachiever and/or do you think no matter what you do it is never enough?

Do you find that you seek or desire acceptance and/or approval from people, and/or that you have a hard time saying "no"?

Do you find that you are always questioning your own judgments and/or actions, and/or do you scrutinize yourself over small faults?

Do you think you are not good enough, stupid and/or worthless or that people are always judging you in a negative way?

Do you hide your feelings and/or opinions from people for fear of being judged negatively, and/or do you feel like a burden to others with your problems?

Within your family and/or circle of friends are you considered "the strong one" who everyone will come to with problems, and/or you never seem to talk much about your own?

Do you think life would be better and/or people would like you more if you were thin/thinner?

Do you find yourself often comparing your appearance and weight to others, strangers and/or models and actors, and wishing to be as "nice looking" or as "thin" as they are?

Do you continuously feel that you are overweight even though others have told you that you are not?

Do family members and/or friends often express concern for your weight-loss/gain, your appearance, and/or your eating habits?

Do you think everyone's problems are more important then your own, or do you belittle your own emotions and pain?

Do you often feel numb or empty inside, like your life lacks fulfillment and happiness, like something is missing or there is a void inside?

Do you feel as though you have a "conscience" or "voice" that tells you negative things about yourself, convinces you that you do not deserve to eat and/or to be happy, or that tells you that you are or deserve to be fat and ugly?

Examining yourself and how you feel, do you believe that you may suffer from anorexia, bulimia or compulsive overeating, or any combination of the three?

Do you suffer from bouts of depression, hopelessness, and/or lack of motivation; and/or do you find your own problems overwhelming and hard to handle?

Are you depressed, suicidal, stressed-out, and/or fatigued; and/or do you suffer from anxiety or panic attacks, mood swings, rage and/or insomnia.

Have you ever been diagnosed with clinical depression, attentive deficit disorder, manic depression, bipolar II disorder, post traumatic stress disorder, obsessive compulsive disorder, or dissociative identity disorder, or any other psychological/neurological illness?

Behaviors

"Purging" is defined as any behavior used to try to rid the body of food, (and sometimes feelings)- this includes self-induced vomiting, restriction and starvation or fasting periods after binging, compulsively exercising, taking laxatives or diuretics, etc.

Do you eat, self-starve or restrict, binge and/or purge, and/or compulsively exercise when you are feeling lonely, badly about yourself or about a situation, or when you are feeling emotional pressures?

While eating, self-starving, or binging and/or purging do you feel comforted, relieved, like emotional pressures have been lifted, or like you are in more control?

Do you feel guilty following a binge and/or purge episode, after eating or during and/or after periods of restriction/self-starvation?

When eating do you ever feel out of control or like you will lose control and not be able to stop; and/or do you try to avoid eating because of this fear?

Do you typically feel guilty after a binge, or after any snack or meal, and like you have almost instantly gained weight, like you are a failure, and/or like you have sabotaged yourself?

Do you use self-starvation, purging, diet pills, laxatives, diuretics, and/or obsessive exercise as a way to attempt to lose weight?

Do you drink a lot of water, tea or coffee, eat a lot of candy or junk food and/or gum, smoke, and/or take caffeine pills as an attempt to control appetite and/or feel more energetic?

Do you abuse alcohol, drugs or prescription medication, and/or practice in self-hurting behavior such as cutting?

Do you weigh yourself often and does the number on the scale dictate your mood and/or self-worth for the day; and/or do you find you are continuously trying to get that number lower?

Are you constantly "on a diet", and/or counting calories and fat grams; and/or do you feel like you've tried every "fad diet" or "lose weight quick" scheme?

Do you set weight-goals for yourself only to find when you reach it that you want to lose more?

Do you do any of the following: hide and/or steal food, laxatives and/or diet pills; eat and/or exercise secretively; avoid eating in public or around others; wear clothes that hide your weight; and/or make excuses (like "I don't feel well) to avoid meals?

Are you secretive about your eating practices, do you think they are abnormal, and/or would you avoid recommending your methods to a family member or friend?

Would you worry about a friend or family member that came to you with similar weight-loss/coping methods?

Do you lie about your eating behaviors, hide them from others at all costs, and/or would you lie or steal to see they could continue?

Do you use self-injury (cutting yourself, burning yourself, pulling out your own hair) as a way to cope with things?

Do you spend a lot of time obsessively cooking for others or reading recipes, and/or studying the nutritional information on food (calories, fat grams, etc.)?

Do you do one or more of the following harmful eating disorder behaviors?

- Restrict food intake or starve yourself (eat very little, eat nothing, or try to eat as little as possible);
- Binge (eat large quantities of food in a short period of time)
- Purge (use methods such as self-induced vomiting or laxatives to attempt to "get rid of" what you've eaten);
- Compulsively overeat (eat even if you are not hungry)
- Compulsively exercise (exercise too much, too vigorously, or where it is intrusive in your life);
- Take diet pills, laxatives, diuretics or other pills or harmful substances to help you curb appetite or assist in purging;
- Chewing/Spitting (putting food in your mouth, chewing it up and then spitting it out -this is another form of binging/purging)

This series of questions may help you determine if you are a compulsive overeater. As set out by Overeaters Anonymous.

Are You a Compulsive Overeater/Food Addict?

1. Do you eat when you're not hungry?

2. Do you go on eating binges for no apparent reason?

3. Do you have feelings of guilt and remorse after overeating?

4. Do you give too much time and thought to food?

5. Do you look forward with pleasure and anticipation to the time when you can eat alone?

6. Do you plan these secret binges ahead of time?

7. Do you eat sensibly before others and make up for it alone?

8. Is your weight affecting the way you live your life?

9. Have you tried to diet for a week (or longer), only to fall short of your goal?

10. Do you resent others telling you to "use a little willpower" to stop overeating?

11. Despite evidence to the contrary, have you continued to assert that you can diet "on your own" whenever you wish?

12. Do you crave to eat at a definite time, day or night, other than mealtime?

13. Do you eat to escape from worries or trouble?

14. Have you ever been treated for obesity or a food-related condition?

15. Does your eating behavior make you or others unhappy?

Have you answered yes to three or more of these questions? If so, it is probable that you have or are well on your way to having a compulsive overeating problem. We have found that the way to arrest this progressive disease is to practice the Twelve-Step recovery program of Overeaters Anonymous.

Overeaters Anonymous is a fellowship of individuals who, through shared experience, strength and hope, are recovering from compulsive overeating. They welcome everyone who wants to stop eating compulsively. Our primary purpose is to abstain from compulsive overeating and to carry this message of recovery to those who still suffer. We have OA meetings that are bulimia and exercise focus.

If you are anorexic or have bulimia you made need professional help or even hospitalization to fully recover.

"Honesty is the first chapter in the book of wisdom."
— Thomas Jefferson

Chapter 7
Solutions for Recovery

He who conquers himself has won a greater victory than he who conquers a city.
—Proverb

People commonly perceive addicts as so deep into their disease of addiction that they do not have periods desiring sobriety. But this couldn't be further from the truth. Addicts, like you and me, have moments of clarity and self-awareness. They have periods when they come face-to-face with the consequences of their illness. They feel guilt, remorse, frustration and even fear. Deep down, most of them do not intentionally set out to inflict emotional pain on their loved ones. They make plans to change. They make promises to be better even if it is only to themselves. The problem is that they cannot keep them. The dynamics of addiction, as we discussed in the previous chapters, add to this difficulty to change.

"I tried. God knows I tried. But I am stuck in this rut. I cannot do anything."

Addiction is a disease that is often associated with a grueling road to recovery. Those who have found themselves dependent on a substance or a self-defeating behavior often experience cycles of attempts to heal themselves and painful relapse. In fact, the road to recovery may in itself be traumatic: full of frustration and self-loathing.

Recovery is possible, there is hope! A good number of people have found help and support and they have moved on to live full and tempered lives. Many have found healing from addictive behaviors as an entry point to healing other things in their lives: healing their personal life, their relationships with family and friends and an improved school and work ethic. But what is clear is that recovery is a process. You cannot change addictive behavior overnight. It may require from you commitment and tenacity but a clean and sober life will be well worth it.

An Ounce of Prevention is Worth a Pound of Cure

Before I begin and discuss with you some suggestions for recovery, I want to emphasize to you a very important fact that is true in most of the risks we take: Prevention is better than cure. You need not always learn via the school of irreparable mistakes. If you are still within experimenting stage, wake up, STOP and catch yourself in time!

Know if you are at risk
Addiction-prone Personalities

Some people are more at risk than others to develop addictions, and it is important that you recognize in yourself whether you may fall prey into this disease. If you are a high risk for addiction, it is best to not even attempt to try something addictive even if you only plan to partake of it in moderation. DON'T START!

Some of questions that may help you assess if your personality is prone to addiction are:

Am I capable of feeling all kinds of emotions i.e. sadness, anger, strength, weakness, love? Is there a particular emotion that I have more difficulty experiencing compared to others? If so, what in my experience has made handling this emotion particularly intolerable?

Do I constantly crave attention, affection, approval and affirmation from others? What happens to me when I do not get it?

Do I often feel like I am a failure? Do I find it difficult to find something in myself to like or appreciate?

Do I have difficulty in sharing myself with other people? Do I often find myself being too scared to be close to someone for fear of being rejected?

Do I have a problem saying "no" to people? Am I the type who would bend over backwards to please others? Am I a people pleaser?

Do I do things for others at my own expense?

If your answer to at least one of these six is yes, you might have a tendency to have an addiction. It would be helpful to find out what are the things that are blocking you be a fully emotionally integrated person.

A Family History of Addiction

One of the most reliable determinants of tendency towards addiction is family history. Most people who develop an addiction come from families who have struggled with some kind of dependency before. While concrete scientific results are still forthcoming regarding the isolation of the "addiction gene," most experts in the field point to a strong influence of heredity. I don't think it is by chance that my family history of addiction resulted in my own and son's addictions. It is a fact that daughters of alcoholics (which I am) if they do not become alcoholics themselves (I don't drink) can become sugar addicts. The reason in that sugar in food or alcohol becomes ethyl alcohol in the system. So I have the same addiction as my dad, he drank his sugar, and I found mine in the form of Oreo's!

My son has pointed out that I can't "get arrested" for having an open bag of Oreo's in the car and he is right but I have fought my addiction just as fiercely as the next addict.

Even if it's not genetic, addiction may be passed across generations socially. When a family has an addicted family member, almost always the results are dysfunctional coping among those around them—coping that predisposes them to develop addictions themselves. I mentioned to you in the first chapter the term codependency. Families of addicts are codependents—this means that in some fashion or another they are addicts themselves. Literally, codependence means *"dependence with."*

Codependency starts this way: Addicts, by nature of their disease, are people difficult to control. However, because you love your family members, you cannot help but try to control them—you do not want them to fall into danger. You might therefore end up trying all kinds of behaviors to get them to change: you might nag them, you cajole, beg, threaten, you call others for help—you might exhaust all means possible. But because they have already lost the power to choose what they want to do with their life, or their addiction is running them, no amount of our effort will get them to change. Our behavior can become just as crazy and insane as that of the addict in our attempt to get them to see "the light." Trust me when I tell you I speak from crazy codependant experience.

If you cannot change your loved ones, you may just end up adapting to them. You can end up coping with the consequences of their drinking in ways that would minimize the pain that you feel. Some people adapt by trying to be a comic, others by burying their noses at work and school, others overeating or drinking themselves.

But certainly we would find a way to distract ourselves rather than own up to what is going on inside of us.

Codependency opens you to become an addict as well because your family situation has made you grow up oriented to the outside rather than inside. You are always looking out rather than in. Think of it this way: It's like having a young child grow up with nothing but an entertaining television as company; the only difference is this time the TV show is one's real life. A child who grows up with a crisis right under his nose never grows up knowing anything about himself: who he is, what he wants, how he feels. He can't, there are always more pressing things to attend to outside. He can't attend to the feelings as well because it is too painful—and it never ends. If you grow up this way, you would develop the instinct that if something is painful, the best way to deal with it is to change the channel on TV—find something else to keep your mind off the drama about to unfold.

Codependency is a condition experienced not just by people who live with addictions but people who live with needy people in general, or people whose needs extra care and support. If you have at least one "colorful character" in your household, or someone you have been trained from childhood to "sacrifice" for, chances are you may develop an addiction yourself. That, plus the fact you may be only able to model what you saw around your family. You might think excessive drinking is "normal" because that is normal in your household. It was no accident that I married another alcoholic after growing up with one I had no idea what "normal" was.

If you live with a particularly difficult parent, you may want to check on their own history with their own parents. Often, if they grew up as codependents, they may unknowingly be passing on some of their repressed emotions to you. Understanding their history can help you look at them more compassionately. More so, if they are willing to get help, you may break the cycle of addiction in your family.

In sum, if there is an addiction your family, you are likely to become an addict yourself. The kind of addiction you inherit/ imitate/ develop need not be directly the same as your addicted family member's. You may have an alcoholic for a parent, but develop a gambling addiction or an eating disorder. But though the object of the addiction is different, the dynamics are the same.

Educate Yourself

Whether you are at risk or not, make sure that you educate yourself. Know all the facts about addiction. Know the signs. Know your trigger points. Seek a professional or even your college counselor to look for more information.

Intervention

In a perfect world an addict would see that their addiction is destroying their life and all those around them. Since the very nature of addiction is denial an addict, despite all the signs around him pointing to his addictive disease, will not admit that he has a problem. The stigma associated with an admission of addiction is one of the things that maintain denial.

I suppose it may be said that addiction thrives on some degree of arrogance. Addicted people think that they have the ability to control a disease, that they are the master of their addiction, when the fact is that they are the ones enslaved by it.

For family and friends waiting for you to hit *your* bottom and go for help may mean staring at you in a casket at the funeral parlor. *Your* bottom and *their* bottom (putting up with your out of control addict behavior) may be two entirely different events.

The most likely scenario is that your family and friends that love and care about you will sit you down, confront your behavior and have an intervention (hopefully with a health professional) and tell you to go into treatment or else! The "else" meaning they will cut off all ties with you and you will face all the consequences of your addiction completely alone. If it means living on the streets or in your car living on peanut butter so be it! It is not usually the case that an addict wakes up one day and says I think I want to go to treatment today!

Breaking Through Your Denial-Addiction Kills

You might find yourself sitting in a rehab and still be bargaining with the addiction. Breaking through denial is not just about gaining awareness that you have an addiction. You also have to OWN the fact that you have a problem, say outright to others that you have a problem. This is important because you cannot do anything about a problem unless you acknowledge that it exists. After all, what is there to cure if you are not ill, right?

Owning your addiction—admitting that you are an addict—is tantamount in humility and a new kind of surrender. It is saying: I need help. I cannot control it anymore. I can't do this alone. This is why denial is often conceived as the most difficult stage: it involves intense feelings of shame, guilt, self-loathing and helplessness. But these are emotions that are necessary to mobilize an addict out of his self-defeating cycle.

How can you break denial? The best way to assess whether you are addicted or not is to look at the consequences of your behaviors. Have you started to miss school? Have your grades deteriorated? Are you having problems in your relationships with others? Are you having health complications? Have you been confronted by family or friends about how you act? Are you having trouble with the law? If you wake up in hand-cuffs in a prison cell chances are good....you have a problem!

Solicit the opinion of others this is of course if you have not been intervened on by this point. After all, in the grips of an addiction we cannot be expected to be objective about ourselves. I suggest you gather the people who are close to you or have close associations with you to give you feedback. Chances are, what the majority of your loved ones say about you is more accurate than what you think about yourself.

More so, let your loved ones speak to you about what they notice about your behavior and how they feel about it. Sometimes it is the knowledge that we have hurt the people who matter to us the most that can jolt us awake with respect to what we are doing.

Physical Recovery

Addictions are physical diseases, as well as emotional, mental and spiritual diseases. Because of tolerance, the physical aspect of addictions needs to be addressed first—one must remove the abusive substance inside the body. This stage is often referred to as detoxification; a stage when the addict is not immediately, or eventually allowed to consume the substance.

The detoxification stage is very important. You cannot work on the mind and the emotions unless the drugs and alcohol have been flushed out of one's system. Nothing can be accomplished with a person who is still on a "high" or has drugs in their body. To do so may even be counterproductive as some substances are psychogenic in nature, meaning they can influence mood and perception.

Physical recovery is as important in cases of eating disorders, where a person may have already caused his or her body considerable damage already as it is with drugs and alcohol. Physical welfare takes priority over other interventions and often concentrated time has to be invested in consultation with medical professionals to have to get a healthy weight back.

In cases when the addiction is not yet in its chronic stages, or when the admitted addict is really determined, physical recovery may be done without a person checking himself inside a rehab center. Some do this by going cold turkey—immediately stopping use of a forbidden substance. Others by gradually lowering doses of a substance until a person is weaned off of it. Because addictions can severely damage a person's physiology, it is best not to do a detoxification program without professional assistance.

Processing Our Personal Issues

Self-reflection and self-assessment is an integral part of the recovery process. This step involves getting in touch with your feeling about yourself and your life and facing the things you have avoided before. This is commonly done through a counseling session, with the help of a trained mental health professional.

Commonly, the struggle of addicts is loneliness. Not a loneliness in the traditional sense of the word; it is not about being physically away from other people. Rather it is loneliness within the presence of others. It is loneliness that is defined as (1) not having our emotional needs met even by those you currently have in your life and (2) not being able to provide for these needs yourself. For regardless of what age you may be, or what your status in life is, at the end of the day we all desire one thing, and that is to feel loved. We need what people call the 3A's: acceptance, affection and affirmation.

Your quest as a young-adult whether you realize it or not is to develop your identity (who you are) and your autonomy (what you can do on your own). Both of these things, however, require an experience of secure and consistent love in order to develop.

Identity is not about what your name is, what you want to be when you grow up or what is your favorite band and movie. Rather identity is 'knowing for certain that you are a person *deserving* of love'. You may know what your dream job is or your favorite color but if you do not feel that you are deserving of love, you will always be looking for who you are. Identity is being able to say that you have worth and value in this world and you do not have to buy or work at anyone's attention, approval or affection. When your identity is in the inner security that you are loved, you do not need things outside of your-selves like expensive clothes and famous friends to validate your value. Your confidence never fluctuates, because it is independent of what is going on around you.

Autonomy on the other hand is not just about what you can get away with now that you are an adult or what you can accomplish without anyone else at your back. It is not about getting your own apartment, being able to drive, or being able to work your way through college. These things help, yes, but autonomy primarily is the felt security of knowing that you have a stable and loving base to always go back to should you fall. You are not afraid to explore and move away—and risk failure!—for you have the confidence that even if you mess up, someone would always be waiting for you. You are free to grow, because the ground is stable not quaky. You know you are loved and that no matter what happens you are awaited by this love—and therefore life has meaning.

This journey towards emotional and mental recovery may be conceptualized in the following choices:

I want to move away from:

Debilitating Depression – Only if I were to consistently believe in the illusion that my life is hopeless and I have no choices. I have the choice to determine how I feel.

Debilitating Overwhelm – Only if I were to consistently focus on the belief that I cannot develop a plan of strategy.

Inappropriate feelings of being unloved – Only if I were to consistently focus on the belief that I am unlovable and unattractive.

Inappropriate feelings of rejection – Only if I were to consistently focus on the illusion that people can reject me instead of realizing that I am the only person who determines how I feel.

Debilitating Anger – Only if I were to consistently treat people harshly or reject them instead of realizing that they have different rules and are doing the best they can with the resources they have, its not about me.

I want to move consistently towards:

Health & Vitality – Anytime I treat my body with love and respect. I am Healthy when I acknowledge how healthy I have already become. Anytime I exercise.

Love & Warmth – Anytime I am loving to myself and others. Anytime I notice love from others.

Joyful & Fun & Outrageous – Anytime I can embrace the playful outrageous child inside of me. I am fun. When I find pleasure and joy in the process.

Gratitude – I feel grateful for what I have in my life right now. I am grateful I have my talents.

Forgiveness – Anytime I open my heart to others unconditionally and without judgment.

Honesty/Integrity – Anytime I hold myself to my own standard. Anytime tell the truth.

Compassion – Anytime I feel love in my heart for another living being.

Faith – Anytime I believe in myself and others no matter what.

Flexibility – Anytime I achieve an outcome.

Growth – Anytime I stretch myself beyond my comfort zone.

Creativity – Anytime I embrace a different concept or idea.

Courage/Determination – Anytime I believe in myself no matter what. Anytime I stretch myself.

Making an Impact – Anytime I share myself with others anytime my life's work impacts others.

Significance – Anytime I use my unique talents/gifts. Anytime my life's work impacts others.

Contribution – Anytime I give of myself to others for the sheer joy of it.

In recovery you may learn that lost opportunities to feel loved can be recovered. Sometimes it involves educating the people around you on how they can best attend to your needs. This is why counseling for recovering addicts is not just with the individual addict. To be more effective, counseling must also involve the family. Addiction is a family disease. It is the time to teach the entire family how they can better be present for each other.

Chapter 8
When One is Too Much,
and a Thousand is Not Enough

When you think about how good that first hit, first drink, first bet, first smoke, first cookie would taste, remember this: you don't really want ONE drink, ONE hit, ONE of anything. You want more. In fact, you want all the drinks, hits, smokes, and cookies in the known universe up to and perhaps past the point where it threatens your life.

Your Social Support Network– Abstinence & Avoiding Relapse

Another phase of recovery is emotional and mental recovery. Often this involves counseling/psychotherapy and joining support groups. The goal at this stage is to identify underlying issues that may have caused or maintained the addiction in order to make sure that they will not be repeated again. It is also the time to arm the recovering addict with coping styles he should use to prevent a relapse. People who have a strong social and family support system are more successful at staying off cocaine and other drugs than those who do not have a strong network. They also are more likely to get their emotional needs met and to feel satisfied with their lives.

When an addict is committed to living a clean & sober lifestyle or one clean from compulsive overeating or gambling they will experience a loss a grieving period if you will of their primary addiction. No matter how much havoc or trauma the addict's drug or alcohol use or other addictive behaviors caused themselves and loved ones or how grateful that others may be that the using or acting-out has stopped—the addict is going to miss their drug. They are going to miss the distraction, relaxation, intensity and high the behavior or substance offered to them. The addict is going to miss their "easy" way to escape difficult feelings and experiences with a buffer.

They are losing a friend or a mistress that must be replaced with healthy behaviors of people, places or things. An addict is only as healthy as the people they hang out with. If someone is committed to abstinence they will have to have a strong support system of people who are in their corner.

Support groups are also another way towards emotional and mental recovery. One of the most accessible support groups are those which offer 12-step programs. There is the Alcoholics Anonymous (AA) composed of alcoholics who want to stop drinking, Narcotics Anonymous (NA) for drug dependents, Gamblers Anonymous (GA) for compulsive gamblers and Overeaters Anonymous (OA) for people with eating addictions. These programs are completely voluntary. Most of them require no fees to attend.

Self-help groups work because addictions thrive in secrecy and denial. At the onset, self-help groups help you to admit that you are an addict. The more people who know about what you are going through the better. It makes you more accountable for your behavior.

But the good thing about support groups is that you are in an atmosphere of a support and acceptance. The people who are with you in a group are also people who experience the same thing that you do and thus would listen to your story without judgment. There is also comfort in knowing that you are understood and that you are not alone.

What is social support recovery?

Social support is:

- The people in your life giving you emotional support. The people in your life (your network) pulling for you to succeed in recovery

- Emotional support and understanding from others as you struggle with a changed lifestyle and personal growth

- Honest confrontation as you establish a lifestyle of recovery. It consists of compliments on your success, reminders when you deviate, and understanding when you are discouraged and hurting

- A network of relatives and friends who provide positive feedback

- The people in your life accepting no excuses from you, but helping you to maintain your motivation and commitment to recovery

- Physical support from others in restructuring your home, work site, and social life to be more conductive to your recovery efforts

Why is social support network necessary in recovery?

When you are trying to recover without positive reinforcement from your social support system, you often:

- Lose interest in your efforts

- Forget the reason for changing

- Feel like your efforts are meaningless

- Feel like your efforts go un-rewarded

- Lose the motivation to change

- Feel discouraged when you have hit a plateau where your changes are less apparent

- Feel depressed because the changes require to much effort: work that is un-rewarded
- Want to give up since there is no visible change in your life or in the ways others react to you

How far can you allow your social support system to go in your recovery process?

You can give those in your social support system permission to:

- Accept you in your new lifestyle and to continue to reinforce you in these changes
- Give open and honest feedback concerning your progress and efforts to change
- Positively reinforce you for your efforts to change rather than just reinforce the changes yourself
- Assist in monitoring your efforts to change
- Listen and be understanding when you are depressed over an apparent lack of progress
- Point out needed alterations in your lifestyle without complaining, or criticizing
- Compliment your efforts to recover and the resulting changes without overemphasis on the changes themselves

Irrational thinking keeping you from seeking social support in your recovery

- I should be able to do this on my own
- It is a sign of weakness to ask others for help
- It is embarrassing to let others know of my personal weakness
- You should never burden anyone else with your feelings or personal concerns

- People who know a lot about me or my life can take advantage of me
- People are basically self-centered and selfish; they don't really care about me
- I don't need others to help me change my life
- People are always trying to get me to conform to their ways of thinking, acting, and believing
- If I let others know what I am trying to do, they will always be on my back
- I hate to be reminded of things I know I need to be doing for myself

Switching to other drugs a relapse trap door

Many addicts are more than willing to acknowledge that their drug of choice is a problem, but often seem to feel that drinking beer is a birthright which cannot be renounced. These same addicts are bewildered when a binge on beer returns them to active use of their drug of choice. This situation applies equally to the person addicted to alcohol who believes that marijuana is a benign herb with magical healing properties.

Our primary purpose in using intoxicants is to change our state of mind, to make ourselves feel good (or better). Using any intoxicant strong enough to alter our consciousness will eventually make us yearn for our drug of choice.

Now let's take a look at some attitudes that might influence you to substitute one drug for another. Respond to these statements honestly; remember, this is just between you and your addiction.

For problem drinkers and alcoholics

- I feel that I will have difficulty coping with certain problems or moods with drugs.
- I have used marijuana without any problems in the past.
- I've experimented with other drugs without experiencing a craving to use them again.
- I've used sedatives or sleeping pills in the past.
- It bothers me that other people can drink and I can't use anything at all!
- I wonder how I will cope with (sleeplessness, headaches, anxiety, depression, fatigue, worry) without resorting to alcohol, or some other drug.
- I don't consider myself an addict.

For primary cocaine, narcotic, and other drug users:

- I used drugs for a long time before I got in trouble with them.
- Even when my drug use was at its worst, I could (smoke marijuana, drink, take pain pills) without problems.
- I don't consider myself an alcoholic.
- I feel it will be hard to cope with my moods and feelings without some chemical.
- I never used alcohol except in social situations.
- It bothers me to think other people can drink and I can't use anything at all.
- I wonder how I will cope with (sleeplessness, headaches, anxiety, depression, fatigue, worry) without resorting to drugs.

This trap normally begins with two incorrect assumptions. First, that problems with one drug do not put you at risk for problems with another. Second, that using a mood-altering substance will not substantially undermine your ability to avoid a return to other drugs.

Here is a review of the thinking process:

- The relapse questions the need for total abstinence from all mood-changing chemicals. He seeks alternatives to abstinence.

- The relapse points out drugs that do not produce relapse to his drug of choice, such as nicotine and caffeine, and seeks evidence that general prohibition is unjustified.

- Seeks out people who have experimented with drugs and uses their experience as social proof that cheating is ok.

- Emphasizes in his thinking and conversation the positive aspects of his experience with drugs, especially drugs other than his drug of choice, and downplays the negative aspects.

- Aligns himself with those attempting to control use of alcohol or drugs, loses identification with abstinent addicts, and isolates him or herself from recovering addicts.

- Decides to, and then begins to, experiment with controlled use of a drug other than his drug of choice.

- Interprets any success in controlled use of alcohol and/or drugs as proof that total abstinence in not necessary.

- Relaxes external controls; usually goes on a binge and returns to primary drug.

Rationalizing—Watch For These and Similar Phrases in Your Thinking:

- You mean if I had one beer I couldn't stop, and I would be an alcoholic forever?
- I don't crave it…if I were going to relapse wouldn't I have a craving?
- Sure cocaine is bad, but I never had any trouble with booze or pot.
- How can I be addicted to something I never even tried?

Exercises For Avoiding This Trap

This is only one reliable way to avoid this trap: ***practice abstinence.*** Most addicts learn about the need for abstinence through failure. If you are lucky you do this on your own, before you go into treatment.

Danger: Not Practicing Abstinence Trap

Although an addict may acknowledge his addiction he may still seek to conquer the disease instead of surrendering to it, known as "selective denial". In our heart of hearts none of us really want to admit that there is a part of our lives that we have absolutely no control over.

Twelve step groups suggest that we practice total abstinence from drugs and alcohol. This is a ***practical*** suggestion, there is no moralizing connected with it. If you don't have the first drink you can't have the second, third, and on, into oblivion.

Unfortunately, too many addicts don't listen. Many people supposedly in recovery insist on "conducting research" just to see if they can regain control over drugs and alcohol.

Some addicts become obsessed with this issue. As loss of control progresses, they engage in a titanic struggle to assert their will over the disease. Each failure brings another vow to succeed with the next attempt. A classic example of insanity

Insanity is Doing the Same Thing Over and Over and Expecting a Different Result!

Are you struggling with the idea of controlled consumption?

- I was never <u>physically</u> addicted to alcohol or drugs.

- I know I could have really quit on my own I just needed to put my mind to it.

- I suspect many recovering alcoholics have a drink from time to time, even if they don't admit it.

- I believe that some recovering addicts can use certain drugs- marijuana or alcohol, for example- without returning to heroin, cocaine, or something else.

- I feel that I could have gotten away with more drinking or drug use except that it really bothered other people.

- I feel that when I drank too much it was because of the situation I found myself in at the time.

- It's hard for me to understand how <u>one drink</u> could hurt.

- Except for my drinking or drug use, I regard myself as an exceptionally strong-willed person.

- Whenever I've put my mind to something I've been able to accomplish it.

If you agree with some of these comments that you are probably not convinced that you <u>can't</u> drink without losing control and that you are not really an alcoholic.

The emotional tone that surrounds this trap is one of the <u>superficial cooperation making quiet resistance</u> or **compliance without acceptance**. Because this hidden agenda would be challenged if it came to light, the addict surrounds it with secrecy.

The Underlying Assumption: That loss of control begins somewhere **after** the first drink.

Resulting Behavior: You admit to being an addict and understand its adverse affects. You retain the belief that someday you will regain the ability to drink or use certain drugs without problems. Those around you mistakenly assume you are committed to abstinence.

The Second Decision: You **convince** yourself that you will be able to regain control over your drinking or drug use. You seek out reports that indicate this is possible.

Resulting Behavior: You discontinue going to meetings, unless required to, and even then you get nothing out of the experience.

The Fourth Decision: You plan on experimenting with some controlled drinking. This decision is kept secret; since other people would only seek to impose their misguided values on you if they knew of your plans.

Resulting Behavior: You begin drinking or using in carefully selected controlled situations.

The Fifth Decision: You interpret any successful attempt- using with-out loss of control-as evidence that your original idea was correct. And that further experiments would be justified.

Resulting Behavior: More experiments. Over time, the experiments with alcohol or drugs grow more frequent and longer in duration. Eventually, loss of control occurs.

When you think about how good that first hit, first drink, first bet, first smoke, first cookie would taste, remember this: you don't really want <u>ONE</u> drink, <u>ONE</u> hit, <u>ONE</u> of anything. You want more. In fact, you want all the drinks, hits, smokes, and cookies in the known universe up to and perhaps past the point where it threatens your life.

> Cement this phrase into your brain:
>
> # ONE IS TOO MANY, AND A THOUSAND IS NOT ENOUGH!

RECOGNIZE THAT SCIENCE HAS NO CURE FOR ADDICTION.

Remember once you are an addict, you will always have a predisposition to return to your addiction. You cannot say, 'okay I've gone through detoxification, some 12 step meetings and counseling, I can take a few sips of alcohol–why not?' There is no way to restore your ability to drink and use without problems. It's like trying to change a pickle back into a cucumber–the transformation only works one way!

To be an addict in recovery means that from that point on you must engage in a lifetime of a social support system to manage your emotions and cravings so that you can maintain sobriety. Thus for addiction recovery to be successful, remember you can't do it alone.

AGAIN, REMEMBER THAT YOU DON'T WANT ONE DRINK, ETC. You're addicted; you want ALL of it there ever was!

Chapter 9
Stories of Experience
Strength and Hope

"Lets's dare to be ourselves,
for we do that better than anyone else can"
—Shirley Briggs

I had to finally embrace recovery.... for me!

What ever happened to Frankie .....

As I lay on my bunk in the county jail I was looking at my honeymoon pictures taped to my upper bunk. I was just staring at the pictures of my wife. I was thinking to myself, how could I have done this to my marriage...to myself. I was in the last days of my 4-month jail term for failing to pay child support! Four months earlier I gambled away the money. A warrant was issued for my arrest, the police came to the house handcuffed me and took me away!

I shared with you earlier in his book that I started my gambling career on sports betting at Santa Clara University.

After the demise of my first marriage and the loss of my daughter going off with her mom I still did not get it. I thought I could handle my sports betting. My gambling addiction and cocaine use burned through another marriage, and two prison terms. I would lie and manipulate and do whatever it took short of murder to survive and feed my obsessive addictions. I went to prison twice and I would still not surrender the addiction...I could handle this on my own. So I thought...

As I got older I lost the respect of my parents and family from too many lies and borrowing money. My daughter was also sick of my behavior and not taking care of my responsibilities. How could I explain my compulsive behavior to anyone else when I could not even understand myself why I was willing to sell my own soul to bet on sports!

I met my wife, Loree whose smile captivated me. The attraction was definitely there and the chemistry was undeniable. I fell in love with her, but it didn't take too long for my dark side to surface and I tried to hide things so she would not see the real me. The gambling me. Our relationship started to unravel and I told her about my money issues. But they weren't really money issues, they were addiction/gambling issues and I was circling the drain fast.

I wanted to salvage my relationship so I promised her I would start attending gamblers anonymous meetings because I thought I had a gambling problem. But deep down I really don't think I wanted to stop gambling yet. I still wanted it my way.

Even though in my heart I loved this woman my ever-present addictions never allowed us to have a truly honest relationship when I was carrying on a sneaky secret life! I really thought I wanted to change my "old ways" when in reality I was doing it for her and not for me! The grip of this disease is powerful and progressive.

I managed to hide enough that we were married in a beautiful ceremony in late August. In a counseling session a month later my wife and our therapist gave me an intervention and in a few days, practically at gunpoint I was on a plane to Baltimore to enter a gambling rehab center. Again I was doing it for her not me!

I learned in rehab that fantasy football was considered gambling. I had been involved in a fantasy football league with guys that I had played with for over 20 years.

When I returned home from Baltimore I did not head the advice to drop out of the fantasy league and drop my gambling friends. I continued to play on the fantasy league behind my wife's back. I struggled all through the football season then I relapsed by placing a bet on the Super Bowl.

Again I was back on a plane to Baltimore for a two-week "dry out" at gambling rehab but once again it was for her. I knew I wanted to stay married but I still hadn't embraced recovery two years after going to my 1st G.A. meeting. My fantasy was that I could carry on two different lives.

I was still bargaining with doing things my way, my plan, and resenting my wife for it.

I told her again that I was going to G.A. meetings and I really wasn't. I would be at a sports bar, going back to my comfort zone of gambling and having a few beers. It didn't take Loree long to see right through my stories and expose me. I have heard of women's intuition but I'm convinced to this day she has a sixth sense of intuitiveness that is unbelievable and it drove me to the brink of insanity. How she caught me and she busted me every time was too much!

My wife had had it with me she was very close to leaving me. She could no longer handle the fact that I was still not willing at that point to do whatever it took to get well and embrace recovery. But then God stepped in with a different plan. God's plan involved handcuffs and an arrest on non-compliance to pay child support and a face-to-face meeting with the hanging judge. His plan said "I am not giving you the get out of jail card this time buddy you go to jail and sit for 4 months and think about your life"...

My wife took God's side and said "don't call me or write me, sit in jail and figure it out." Do you think my wife would bail me out and not let me sit in jail? Not on your life! Her recovery plan was to let me hit bottom and deal with all the consequences that I created for myself. I had cried wolf too many times.

The members of G.A. wrote to me, visited me in jail and were there for me those 4 months. I was finally willing to drop the rock and embrace recovery. Not just talk about it or BS anyone, but really...do it. Jail humbled me to finally listen. My wife wasn't interested in talking with me unless I was in a program and working on my recovery bottom line. She would not even come to pick me up when I was released from jail. She had heard all my promises before I had worn out that story.

They say there are no accidents...When I was released the following morning I was standing at a payphone with garbage bags of my clothes and I knew that I had to do something different my addictive plan did not work anymore. I then decided to check myself into a 30-day drug & alcohol program to get to the bottom of my destructive addictive patterns. Even though I left cocaine behind 20 years ago on my own I had still smoked pot socially up until 17 months ago. I just wanted a clean life all the way!

In recovery they say there are three outcomes from addiction, prison or institutions (been there done that) insanity (doing the same thing over and expecting a different result) I tried that too! or death (I was still breathing so I had that in my favor). Well I chose a fourth outcome...recovery!

I am now clean, sober and abstinent from gambling. This

time I am doing this for me! I know this addiction is cunning, baffling, powerful, deadly and patient. I always thought I was a bad person and today I know that I am not a bad person. I have a disease it is called addiction and it is treatable.

I am currently enjoying my wife, as I never have before. I write this with great pride today that it is now great to have my best friend back! My wife has always loved me, it was the addict behavior she hated, not me, and there is a difference. She has supported me in my recovery, and we are working to rebuild trust and a shattered marriage that could have easily gone to divorce court.

I live my life and marriage one day at a time now. Going to jail this last time actually saved not only my marriage but also my life! Without this recovery lifestyle it would only be a matter of time until I went back to jail behind my addictions. I am telling the truth everyday and living an honest program. Today I feel humble and filled with gratitude. It is good to be alive...I couldn't honestly say that before my recovery...

—With peace and love in my heart, Frankie

Family abuse, and a brutal rape drove me into multiple addictions

My father was a raging alcoholic, my mother was emotionally distant and growing up in my household was painful. When I was three years of age, my family was struck with the tragedy of my five-year-old brother's death. He was a disabled boy, with a lot of love for life. Soon after my parents divorced, and I found myself on the witness stand telling a courtroom full of people why I did not want to live with my alcoholic and abusive father.

Then when I was five years old I was molested by my

mother's boyfriend, and to make matters worse, I was returned to live with my abusive father. During this time, when I was repeatedly beaten up, and tortured by my father I began my addiction with food. I lived in a world where I felt that I had no control in what was happening in my life, I learned that the only thing I could control was what I ate. Food was such a comfort to me, and a way of "checking out" of whatever situation I could not emotionally deal with. I was having a really big self-esteem issue, my mothers emotional distance left me feeling like she didn't want me, or my father didn't want me either for that matter, it was very hard on me.

Looking back I had great potential I was a great student, and taking courses to become a teacher! I finished all my high school requirements in my junior year, so my senior year, I took college courses. Because of being caught up in my addictions I never made it.

I started acting out in my teens when my mother and I moved to Seattle, WA. In the state of Washington, gambling is legal. For the first year we lived there, my mother was not home most of the time. I always thought that she was at work. When my step-dad came to live with us, it became more evident that something else was going on. A friend of mine lived near a casino, and my mom would drop me off at her house, and I would get a call five hours later from my step-dad wondering where she was. Or on the other side, she should have picked me up earlier in the day, and wouldn't show up until that night.

My mother would disappear for days at a time, showing up with no explanations for her absence. I can remember when we finally realized where she was going, and why we never seemed to have any money. When she would disappear then, instead of just worrying, now we were calling casinos trying to get her paged to call home. We drove to the local gambling establishments to see if we could drag her out. It was terrible. When I was 16 my mother finally came out about her gambling addiction.

When I was 17 I was kicked out of my home for lying to my mother. I have struggled ever since. I worked two jobs, and lived in really bad neighborhoods, because they didn't have leases. Not being 18 I was very limited as to where I could live. Inevitably, it seemed I never got back on the college path...

Even though I did not start college I swore to myself I would never end up like my mom or my dad with their addictions, I was going to be smarter than that. I was going to stay away from everything that they were addicted to, to not tempt myself in the same situations.

Little did I know at the time, I was headed for the same path. Not only did I have the food addiction, I started to experiment with drugs. My drug of choice for a while was pot, but shortly after I turned 18 another tragedy struck, I was brutally raped.

When that happened, I really wanted to "check out" emotionally more than anything, so I starting smoking crystal meth. This tied into my food addiction. I would not eat for days at a time, but when I did eat, I binged like there was no tomorrow. During those times, I consoled myself by taking a lot of diet pills at once, and then smoking more meth. It was a terrible combination, one that I still regret to this day.

Just after I had started smoking meth, I had someone come to live with me which fed my habit. This person was a crystal meth cook. I got the drugs whenever I wanted it, however much I wanted. In early 2003 something dreadful happened. This person I was living with went crazy, and pulled out a sawed-off shotgun on a group of people. Scared to death I fled the apartment! Soon after, twenty-three squad cars pulled up drawing their guns. The Sheriff approached me in the parking lot, and found that it was my apartment they had in their sights. I gave the Sheriff permission to storm the apartment, and of course when they did, they found more than what they were expecting.

I am very grateful for my friends, everyone I knew there swore to the police that I had no knowledge of the drug, and they let me go. I swore I would never do drugs again! I was given a second chance, and I stuck to my promise. I finally kicked the meth habit in early 2003, and thankfully have not gone back to drugs since. The withdrawals were unbearable! I called my big brother for help, and before I knew it, I was on a bus from Seattle, WA to Santa Rosa, CA. A new beginning... so I thought....

Then came in my gambling addiction. When I gave up one addiction I replaced it with another. Most of us do. My gambling was progressive. I started going every now and then. But in a very short time it turned into everyday. I lived to gamble! I could not wait to go back to the casino!

It caught up to me though, and very quickly. I was facing living on the streets again, with no help from anyone, and no job. That was my bottom and I sought recovery. Without recovery I don't know where I would be today. It has changed my life in so many ways! Recovery has helped me to cope with all of my addictions.

In recovery, I have learned that even though I may not be able to control what's going on around me, I have two choices. One, I can just accept the situation for what it is and move on, *or two, I can let the situations run my life instead of me guiding my own. I don't let addictions or situations run my life any longer and I take life one day at a time.*

—Marlene G.

Compulsive Gambling was Supposed to Happen to Me...

I can see that now, after three years in recovery, which means not placing a bet, attending meetings, getting involved with the fellowship of Gambler Anonymous, and living "one day at a time."

Like many others, I was forced to enter Gamblers Anonymous by my spouse. At first I attended meetings to appease her. Asking for help, and working on myself was something that I had to learn. I believed that everyone else was the problem and that "if" they changed; all my problems would be solved. I was wrong. The world will not change to meet my desires.

It all began when I started gambling in elementary school. Marbles was the game and getting all of the marbles on the playground was the aim of the game. I wanted the prettiest and the most. In high school, sports, and in college: running the pools with my buddies was the way to stay in action. I believed that everything was under control.

I seemed to have crossed the line, if there really is a line, when I started to believe that I could afford to gamble. I always had access to more money. Money became something that I believed could be created and dreamed up. I was smarter than everyone else. I knew that.

The consequences did not matter. There were no bound-aries. Actual loses, and there were lots of loses, were only con-quered with thoughts of winning and having a larger amount of money. I believed that "if" I had more money, lots of it, then all my problems: love, work and school would be solved.

My behavior was compulsive, and addictive and, everyone else was to blame. Gambling was only a problem when I lost. But, when I won, it was not enough, and when I lost it was someone else's fault.

I had no responsibility. I would be ridin' high on my latest win, and all the while I was emotionally and spiritually bank-rupt. I was addicted to the "action" and the risk that placing a bet generates. My attachment to the power of money drove me to desperation.

I was always panic stricken on the inside, but tried to show the world a calm, cool and collected exterior. I was a mess and the only person that I was fooling was myself.

Why did I gamble? I learned that taking a calculated risk was easier than working for a living. Gambling was easy. I stayed away from cards. I knew that the cards and the slot machines were stacked against me. Sports, pro and college, could not be manipulated like a slot machine, or a deck of cards. I was wrong....

—Will N.

"In the middle of difficulty lies wisdom"
—Albert Einstein

A heroin addict puts his life back together

"Conquering any difficulty always gives
one a secret joy, for it means pushing back a
boundary-line and adding to one's liberty."
— Henri Frederic Amiel

I started using heroin when I was 18 years old. I was a base player in a start-up band and had friends that were habitually snorting it. They told me that it would "help me be more creative" and "play my guitar better." When I first tried it I did feel more prolific. It was like something in my head snapped and I opened myself to my muse.

At the beginning, I was only snorting it. I loved the way it made me feel. I felt like I could do anything, I was at the top of my game. It made me feel confident too—I took risks with my guitar playing that I didn't before—and the crowd seemed to love it.

I wasn't worried about getting addicted. At the beginning Jeremy, my band's lead vocalist, oriented me at the onset the difference between addiction and recreational use. He said that the occasional snorting of heroin is no different from eating cake. I was giving my body a small amount of something that while has no nutritional benefits, gives it pleasure—no different from taking sugar. I believed him of course. He was much older and I thought cooler than I was. I started joining my band in using heroin during our weekend practices. At that time we were not even spending anything for the stuff. A dealer in the club we played at "liked us" and supplied us for free. I didn't know at the time that "free drugs" were just a marketing gimmick by dealers to initiate you to a drug. Once you are addicted, they have created for themselves long term clientele.

Once a week was not enough. I felt like I needed a fix on the long days in between practices. The euphoria was all that I could think about. To make matters worse, my weekend fix wasn't making me happy anymore. I hooked up with the dealer who was supplying us and asked if he had extra drugs. He told me it will cost me. I asked him how much. When he told me I didn't even flinch. I had the money, no problem. Could he wait while I make an ATM run? He could. I was happy.

It wasn't long before I started using it everyday. I wasn't just snorting it either. I went the direct-to-the bloodstream route: I was shooting it up with a syringe. Soon after I was also mixing heroin with cocaine. The combination brought me an unspeakable thrill.

My parents did not notice anything that had changed. But then, our household was like a motel. Family members coming and going but barely talking to one another. Everybody usually just minded their own business. One day though, my uncle from my mother's side visited us. He is a policeman and took one look at me and declared that something was wrong. He asked me point-blank in front of my parents: are you using drugs? I said "no." He didn't believe me. My parents didn't either. They took me to be tested. When the results came back positive, I was sent to my first drug rehab center. I stayed for three days. Then I walked out and crashed at Jeremy's place. Suffice to say, it was back to the habit again.

My parents found me at Jeremy's but did not ask me to come home. They said I was old enough to decide for myself and if this is the route that I had wanted to take for myself, if it was then I should live with the consequences. They cut me off from my allowance and ATM.

The gigs we were playing weren't paying that well and after a while became far and few in between. With no allowance and no adult friends I did not have any more money to buy drugs. The dealer would not let me have drugs on credit. I started to go through withdrawals. I couldn't sleep or eat. I felt like I was going crazy. In one moment of complete desperation, I tried to inject my veins with air. I didn't even consciously want to commit suicide; I just needed to try something–anything–that might get me through the withdrawal. Jeremy found me. Because he was a drug user like myself, what I tried to do to myself scared him. He called my family. My Dad picked me up in thirty minutes. He started to cry, which was difficult to take for he was a big guy with not an emotional bone in his body. But as we drove home he begged me to get help.

He enrolled me to another rehab, a more expensive one than the last time. I got clean and sober for three weeks after. I went home and for awhile we were happy. We made plans; my parents were going to enroll me in a music academy so that I would stay engaged in something that I loved to do. It was a great idea. Except for one problem, I had friends in the academy that are within the same circle of my drug using friends. It wasn't long until I saw my dealer again. I got back in the drug game.

My parents in tears told me to get help or get out. I chose the latter, I was so ashamed of myself but too proud to get help—again. I was hurting myself and ashamed of what I was doing but I produced a brave front. I pretended I didn't care that I was booted out of my own house. I pretended to have no emotions.

I went to live on the streets. I learned to live a life of crime. A particular gig that paid me rather handsomely enough to support my habit was male prostitution. There were several occasions were I was caught, but I easily got out. It seemed the club where I worked had some awesome connections in the local police department.

One day I overdosed. I woke up with cold water being poured over my head and being slapped about by a gay customer. I saw my life flash before my eyes. I started crying. I didn't want to go on living the way I was living anymore. I called my parents to come get me. For good measure I called my uncle that was the policeman. When I saw him we were both worn out. My absence had also taken its toll on him and I later found out, my parents' marriage.

I went to another treatment facility but this time my heart was in my goal. I wanted to stay sober I was determined and I followed all that the staff told me to do. I got a sponsor. I started working through the steps. I got honest with myself.

I told myself, my body would betray me. It will crave. It will make things painful for me. But I have my head. I will mentally steel myself for this. I wrote a song about the life I wanted to have. I sing it when I struggle with relapse. I thought of my parents to whom I have to make so many amends to. I keep in my memory the disgusting feeling of waking up naked in a gay customer's house after prostitution and overdose.

Since that day, I have been sober. I have not used for almost 4 years now. For a heroin addict like me, that is a complete miracle. I returned to the music academy. I am putting my life together again.

—Jensen

The destruction of dishonesty...

My name is Gary and I am a compulsive gambler in recovery.

Gambling was an acceptable behavior when I was growing up. As a kid I watched my parents, grandparents, and cousins, bet on playing cards, bet on pool, bowling, and even monopoly. By age 14 or 15 we were allowed to gamble and bet with my aunts and uncles.

As I entered my mid 20's I was introduced to what was called casino gambling by my first wife's uncle Mariani at Joe's card club in San Jose. It was 5-card draw poker $5 was the buy in. As we were leaving early that morning after playing cards all night I asked uncle Mariani what is this other game on the table he said "you don't want to know." Of course I wanted to know so I went back to Joe's card club where I got introduced to low ball gambling. That game took me on a dark destructive ride for 18 years.

In mid 90's that game was not longer played and I was introduced to Texas hold 'em and then the late 90's to double handed poker. This hand was very fast and for a compulsive gambler that provided that adrenaline powered addiction rush. Double handed poker was the fastest money making game in Casino cards rooms.

The game feed my addiction to the full extent. I developed the big shot high roller self-delusional behavior that fed my compulsive gambling. This game has destroyed hundreds of thousands of peoples of lives I was going down in flames and my life was a mess. The behavior and the code of conduct of my compulsive gambling became unbearable for me to live. In the root of all my sickness was the dishonesty to myself, my wife, family and my friends. The compulsive lying was becoming too much for me to bear. I was on a very long and destructive ride.

It got to a breaking point at 2007. I needed to make some changes. When I went to another program and got sober I had to address the truth of my gambling and dishonesty. As I began to attend a 12-step program of rigorous honesty I met a gentleman with 21 years sobriety. We talked for several hours and I shared my gambling history and his response was "you don't have a gambling problem you have a dishonesty problem. That was the beginning of my freedom I did not want to lie anymore. I showed up in Gamblers Anonymous and my life has changed because of the principles of the program. I live an honest program today and for that I am grateful.

—*Gary C.*

"Less of Me, More of You"

"My name is Joshua, and I am a recovering alcoholic."

Whenever I say this to people, I always get a surprised reaction. My age has a lot to do with the disbelief; I am now 29 years old. Most people presume that alcoholics are a lot older, that it takes at least a lifetime to drown yourself in this disease. Ironically, when I call myself as alcoholic, there are those who think I am exaggerating. But mostly, the shock comes from knowing who my family is. I was the last person on earth anyone would expect to engage in bad behavior.

I came from a solid christian family. My father was Senior Pastor at a local Baptist Church and my mother a full-time housewife. Throughout elementary and secondary education I had been home schooled; my mother attended to me and my four other siblings. We were well respected in the community. Our household was always filled with love and care. There was no reason to produce a black sheep.

At a very early age I've been held to a very high standard of behavior. As a christian I was not encouraged to drink any alcoholic beverage, even a sip. I was also advised that I was not to start a sexual relationship until after I was married. I was to take my body seriously and respect it: I should not put anything harmful inside it nor share it with just anyone. My body was the temple of the holy spirit.

Respect for my body is something that I sincerely believed in. I took my parents' words seriously; I took what I knew to be God's word seriously. It had been easy to account for myself all through my growing up years. Being home schooled I was always under loving supervision and surrounded by friends and family who thought that same way I did. Things became different though when I entered a secular university. There, temptation was harder to overcome.

Everything in college was new to me. I have never been part of a really large institution before and the university I went to was large — had a student population of 55,000! For me, the sheer amount of things I could do in this new environment was overwhelming. Plus I have never really been exposed to a great variety of lifestyles and belief systems. It was an adventure that I could not resist.

My greatest struggle had been trying to fit in with the crowd. I wanted to make friends and be accepted — what college student doesn't? I wanted to enjoy my newfound freedom. I had not realized how restricted I had felt going through my non-traditional education. The faith and manner of living that I grew up with was not what I had chosen, it was something that I had to follow by default — because my parents passed it to me. Thus I suppose christianity was never really anchored deeply in my person. Certainly I had questions *about it, and college was the perfect time and place for me to find others to answer my questions.*

Fitting in was difficult for me. I was too different, or as my acquaintances used to say, too "uptight" and "old-fashioned." I was also rather introverted; I was the type of person who will not talk unless spoken to, the type who is most comfortable fading into the background rather than standing out. I felt that I must be some kind of a freak to be avoided by everyone. It was only later upon reflection did I realize that I was lonely because I chose to be rather than shy and unconfident—but there was nothing wrong with me as a person. It wasn't long before I experienced college as lonely and demeaning.

When recruitment for school fraternities opened that year I began to feel a solution for my problem. Maybe if I joined a fraternity, I would have people whom I could hang out with and things in school would improve. There was one fraternity in particular that was notorious for giving its members a good time. I thought, "what the heck," this may be well worth trying out. I had to go through four initiation rites—harmless stuff, just embarrassing—before I got accepted. But when I did I became part of a community that was a tightly knitted as it could possibly be.

I met a lot of good people in the fraternity; they were good-natured kids who appeared to take their education seriously. They were fun and outgoing and they challenged my social skills. They are also great debaters and I enjoyed sharpening my wit with them from time to time. They were great friends.

Unfortunately they were also the worst influence in my life. This fraternity group drank almost everyday, if not inside dormitories; they drank at the clubs late at night. I was a special target for their ribbing and their challenges too, given my own background. At first I was able to refuse and say no, later though I was giving in more and more and going along with the crowd.

When I entered my sophomore year, my drinking became worse. There was more than one occasion when I blew off my classes to go out and drink the whole day with the fraternity. We kept beer in the dormitories too (it's illegal but the floor assistant was part of our gang) and sometimes alcohol hit my stomach long before food did. Every time I got an inkling that I may want to stop I ended up rationalizing: "I drink, yes, but I am not as bad as so-and-so. He's still okay, so am sure I will be too."

I also met a girl then, a freshman student by the name of Laura. Her roommate was the girlfriend of one guy in the fraternity and so she always hung around with us. She took particular notice of me and asked me out. I was so flattered by the attention—it was all so new—that I said yes to everything she wanted. It wasn't long before we were having sex. If you ask me now I can barely remember how it all went down. I was already drinking at least eight bottles a day at that time and had moments when I woke up in places without having any idea how I got there. I even had a couple of blackouts. My relationship with Laura was a blur. But what was clear to me was that my alcohol consumption doubled when I started dating Laura: I consumed large amounts with fraternity friends and large amounts with Laura.

I suppose the greatest hook that alcohol had over me was that it let out my inhibitions without question. I grew up in an environment where rules are always clear and the mind is always superior to the body. Because I am usually shy and insecure, drinking made me more socially adept.

My parents had no idea of all these changes inside me. They checked on me via phone from time to time but I always was able to concoct one lie after another. I was able to assure them that everything was all right with me, that I was working a hard as I could to get my degree, and there was no reason to drive in to visit. They seemed to believe it.

In my junior year, I was kicked out of the university. Rather than admitting this fall from grace, I put up the pretense that I was still studying. To be with my "friends", I just snuck inside the dormitories. It was a good time for me because I used "tuition money" for my habit and myself.

I carried on this way until two events knocked some semblance of sense in me. The first one was when one of my fraternity friends met with an accident while driving under the influence. The accident had damaged his spine and he became paraplegic. I felt cold all over when I head the news and knew that I had to help myself. I saw my future in my friend lying motionless in the hospital bed. I tried to go cold turkey then, and stayed away from my fraternity friends—but I succeeded for only two days. I couldn't do it. It was too difficult.

My failed attempt at recovery scared me more than anything I had experienced that day. It was at that moment of failure that I got an inkling that the drink was more powerful than I was, that I might not be as 'in control' as I thought I was. The fear was there with me everyday and yet I couldn't stop. I wanted to call my parents and ask for their help but I was too embarrassed. I had absolutely no logical reason to give them when they would have asked me "why?" How could I explain my need? They would not understand, they were hard-core religious people. I had better deal with this on my own. I tried but surrendered anyway.

The second event that jolted me was getting Laura pregnant. I don't know what put me in more shock: when I heard her tell me that she is carrying my child or when she had casually told me that she planned to get an abortion soon. I begged her not to, I told her that I was willing to raise the child with her, but she told me it wasn't debatable. Laura told me there was no way I could stop her, she just wanted me to know before she went to a doctor.

All throughout college, I repressed my identity as a christian. I just wanted to be a regular student and one with the crowd. Deep down I did not feel like I was a christian during the progression of my disease I was killing my faith slowly. I stopped praying and stopped going to church. I thought religion was just a way of thinking my parents passed to me. But when Laura gave me her news I knew that I was lying to myself. Deep down inside myself, my faith was still inside. It became apparent in my sheer horror at the realization that my girlfriend is planning to kill my child.

Laura cannot be convinced to change her decision. That was when I felt the certainty that I needed to ask for help. I did not call my parents to help me before out of embarrassment and fear. But now I knew I needed their help, for my child's sake. I didn't think I would be able to live with myself if I did not do everything in my power to stop Laura from having an abortion. So I called my parents to and told them everything and that I needed their help. For the first time in a really long time, I prayed to God.

My parents cried and cried when they heard what I had to say—they immediately drove to the university. They told me how they had already felt that something may be wrong but decided they would trust me. At first I was defensive: I made my plight to be their fault. But my parents must have been praying real hard. I felt my defenses break. I apologized and allowed myself to be taken to rehab.

My parents were never able to talk Laura or her parents out of an abortion, and that is something that I will carry in my heart forever—a reminder of how moments of irresponsibility can cause the life of another. As for me I committed myself to counseling and AA. When I shared with everyone in my support group that I surrendered my life to a higher Power, I meant it. I fully understood then what it meant to give your life over to the care of God who created you.

I do believe that God has a plan for me. His plan is to be the best I could possibly be. I have to trust His plan, trust it enough to look for it even if it seems so far away. We have to be consistent and attune ourselves to him and nothing else.

I now speak to dozens of young people about alcoholism and life. I have made it my vocation and ministry. I have been sober now for four years.

—Josh

Chapter 10
Take A Leap of Faith-
Let the Magic Begin

"Nothing can bring you peace, but yourself."
—Ralph Waldo Emerson

I have covered so many different facts and possibilities in this book you may be a little overwhelmed. But my suggestion is that you start at the beginning. Start with your heart—that is where it all begins for us as human beings. If your heart is wounded, take a leap of faith and ask for help. If you think all your issues are handled, but you see yourself in these mind games you can play with yourself or find yourself in compulsive behavior trust me—your issues are there like cobwebs deep in your soul. It's time to do some deep soul searching.

First and foremost, be gentle with yourself—you have been living in shame long enough. If you have used drugs, alcohol, engaged in gambling or compulsive eating as a way of coping with your emotions in the past, so be it. Don't be ashamed anymore of who you are. Maybe your addiction was what was available to you when life got hairy and you did not know what to feel. It was the only anesthetic that was available to you.

You have to take the attitude. "I did the best I could with what I knew then now I have better information." That was then, now is now the past does not equal the future.

I have opened my heart to you, and shared some very personal and painful pieces of my life, and that of others, so you can see what complex and emotional beings we truly are. I have shared some of my painful family issues that kept me emotionally immobilized for many years. Now that we have come to the end of our time together, I want to share with you the healing that came come from such a tremendous emotional catharsis.

I shared with you in the beginning of this book the experience of growing up with my dad. Now I decided I did not want the pain from the past to haunt me any longer. I wanted to be emotionally available to my family and out from under this emotional burden. I wanted to share my heart with the only living person still available to me, my dad.

My dad had come from Florida for a visit. I asked my dad to take a walk with me to the park so we could talk privately. I looked at my dad (with softness, not accusation) and said "dad, there are some things I need to share with you about what I experienced in my life growing up with you and mom."

The first thing he said was, "Kiddo, I can tell you that I am not an alcoholic." I said, "dad, my experience has taught me that I grew up in an abusive alcoholic family."

"Dad," I said "I am not here to put blame on anyone. I'm past that, but what I want is for you to hear my experience of certain events in my life that involve you and how it has affected me."

I gained a new found respect for my dad that day. What I proceeded to tell him would not be easy for anyone to hear. The tone in my voice was soft and gentle—not accusatory or emotional. You have to understand that once you discharge the emotional pain of an event you can speak of it without all the emotionalism that was once attached to it. I proceeded to tell him some of the events that I experienced in our family from his abuse and his violitle temper when he was drinking.

The look on his face was like that of a little boy—very sad and ashamed. He honestly did not remember these events. His drinking had caused a lot of blackouts, which is common in alcoholism.

My goal was not to shame him but just speak my truth to him from my heart. Rather than get defensive and argue that these events did not occur, he expressed extreme regret and gently said," Honey, I am so sorry."

"I know you are, dad—no one wants to intentionally hurt his family" I said. "But the disease of alcoholism can take on a life of its own and tear up everyone in its path. Your drinking hurt me. It hurt our family."

He then admitted that he knew he had a "drinking problem" and had actually sought counseling in the years after my mother and he divorced. I feel grateful that he took care of himself to heal his wounds with a counselor.

My dad and I came to a healing that day out in the park and in the fresh air. Father and daughter shared thoughts and feelings that had been locked up for what seemed like a lifetime. I forgave my dad that day. I forgave my dad, as my father, a man that carried his wounded inner child deep within his heart.

Yes, I wish had grown with the Ozzie and Harriet family, but I didn't, and forgiveness is a powerful tool.

"If you think you can't...you must"
—Anthony Robbins

I am sure you remember the movie the Wizard of Oz? You'll find like Dorothy did that you have the power to go home to your authentic self anytime you choose, you just didn't know it. Dorothy didn't know clicking her ruby heels three times would get her back home to Kansas. Dorothy took a long treacherous journey down the yellow brick road, just as many of you have just to find out the great Wizard of Oz was an imposter—like addictions of alcohol, drugs or gambling. Addictions set you up to be an imposter in your own life hiding and leading a double life like the wizard behind the curtain.

I wish I could tell you to just click your heels three times and your addiction will disappear but who would I be kidding. Healing your life won't be as instantaneous as clicking your heels or a magic wand passing over your head, but now you have the tools and the missing puzzle pieces to put them together. Because you are unique, you will have your own unique combination of pieces that will make this all fit. The good news is this—if you follow the yellow brick road you will come home to yourself. You may have been missing much longer than you were aware of.

Encouragement

"I have never seen a person grow or change in a constructive direction when motivated by guilt, shame, and/or hate"
—William Goldberg

We all need encouragement to stretch ourselves to behavior that at first seems uncomfortable. If you were teaching a young child how to ride a new bike, you would be patient when the child didn't get it on the first try. You can count on it, it will take many attempts for a child to fully learn how to ride a bike. You would encourage that child and say "come on— you can do it!"

It's the same with you; you're learning behaviors that are different. You may feel emotionally wobbly (the same as the child on a bike) as you get your emotional balance. You may need encouragement from others to help you realize you *can do it.* This may come in the form of a support group that deals with your specific issues. If you are a compulsive food addict, gambler, drug abuser or alcoholic then a support group such as 12-Step Anonymous programs may give you the encouragement you need. There are many groups with therapists also this is just an example.

There is tremendous healing in knowing that you are not alone in your issues. Knowing others are struggling with the same feelings and issues that you do helps you realize that you are human just like they are. Support groups can give you tools to encourage yourself and help you with acceptance.

Have you ever felt so bad that you just wanted to pull the covers over your head and stay in bed and hide from the world for a day, a few weeks, or months? Inside you feel discouraged, hanging out with your two best friends *whiney* and *poor me?* You long for a shoulder to cry on, someone to love and support you, (sniffle, sniffle), someone to give you the encouragement to go on.

We all long for this kind of support, for the knowledge that you have a loving, caring, nurturing parent behind you, encouraging you, telling you...*you can do it!* When you support yourself, you are being this kind of loving parent to yourself, assuring yourself that no matter what happens, you always come home loved. Encouraging yourself is letting you know that no matter how bad things get, no matter what losses or disappointments you may suffer, you always have yourself in your corner for encouragement and support.

Recovery of Your Self-Esteem

"No one can make you feel bad about yourself, without your permission"
—Eleanor Roosevelt

Young adults are especially vulnerable to feeling inadequate and depending on the approval of others for their self-esteem. Codependency, which we discussed earlier, also involves getting your sense of self-worth from the approval of others, rather than generating it from within yourself. It is therefore not surprising that so many of you have limited or fragile self-esteem. If this is your problem, you can learn to value yourself for who you truly are.

I believe that this is exactly the mindset that leads many of you to overeat, drink, gamble, use drugs or participate in other compulsive behavior as a last-ditch effort to nurture yourself. If you are not giving yourself the respect you deserve, addictions can become an emotional crutch. Then you feel guilty, lose respect for yourself, and start the self-critical cycle all over again.

This self-punishment doesn't work, and in fact even backfires thereby lowering your self-esteem even more making you feel hopeless. The only solution you often come up with is to criticize yourself. This self-perpetuating cycle where self-perceived failure leads to self-belittlement, which further decreases self-esteem. Low self-esteem produces feelings of hopelessness and despondency, which sap your energy and faith needed to strive and achieve, thus producing more failure. Does this sound familiar to you? Do you think whatever you do is just not good enough? Do you *awfulize* and hold yourself to a seemingly impossible standard?

"Guilt is I made a mistake...
Shame is I am a mistake"
—John Bradshaw

You may use your achievements as a way to value yourself. This can be a set-up, because sometimes no matter how much you achieve, you may feel that it is never enough. Often, despite receiving the respect and admiration of others, you may feel like an imposter inside— afraid to expose your real deficiency. You look at each achievement as something that only increases others' expectations of you, and that sets you up for a harder fall when your unworthiness is revealed. You many long to feel content and pleased with yourself, but self-contentment is the one thing you cannot achieve.

Self-esteem is an inside job. It can come only from the inside, from inner acceptance and approval. If this self-approval is not there, then the effects of outside commendation and rewards last only as long as the compliments keep coming in. When they cease, you may suffer a dramatic drop in self-esteem, you may become depressed. To be truly anchored in feelings of self-worth, you need to approve of yourself for who you are.

*"Somehow we learn who we really are
and then live with that decision."*
—Eleanor Roosevelt

Here are some nurturing acts and attitudes that will help you grow and flourish.

Compassion

Compassion, when it is genuine, and allows you to take it in as a healing energy that goes directly to where you're hurting, warming and sustaining you. Reach into your heart and think of how if felt when someone was truly caring and compassionate to you. Compassion does not make the problem go away, but you have a much stronger outlook when sharing your concerns and being treated compassionately.

If you were to see a child crying and upset, would you not be compassionate to that child? You would not berate that child when he or she was hurting. Then why would you be any less compassionate to yourself?

Circumstances may not always provide a friendly confidant when problems arise. In that case you can learn to give compassion to yourself. You can learn how to develop an inner voice that is caring and loving, ready to encourage you and give you the courage to go on.

Acceptance

*"Your friend is the man who knows all about you,
and still likes you."*
—Elbert Hubbard, The Notebook, 1927

Compassion goes hand in hand with acceptance. If you respond to yourself with compassion rather than beating yourself up with disappointment, you are accepting yourself as the imperfect human being that you are. Sometimes things just don't go well in our lives or as planned. As the saying goes, *sh*t happens!* It may have nothing to do with you. If your self-esteem depends on external circumstances, then *anything* and *everything* will bowl you over with self-doubt.

You can lean to accept yourself as you are and *to be* there for yourself. We all have problems, and failings, and things we could have handled better, but that does not make us undeserving of caring, empathy, and assistance. How many times have you said to yourself, "I should have done that...I could have done that..." It is the "shoulda, woulda, coulda" syndrome. On the contrary, you need to accept and appreciate yourself as you are, even as you are attempting to improve yourself and your life.

Facing yourself and accepting in a nonjudgmental, nurturing way the things you previously denied or hated about yourself helps you to change these "character defects" into positives. *Not* accepting yourself keeps you stuck.

Learning to accept yourself is something that happens one baby step at a time. As you move forward, there are bound to be old habits and patterns that cause you to step backward at times. Therefore, one of the first things you have to accept is that you are not going to change overnight. Change takes place slowly, and at each step along the way you need to give yourself credit for what you *are* doing, rather than focusing on what you are *not* doing.

When you accept yourself, you start to be close to yourselves and to fill yourselves up. In doing so, you also become more able to accept what others have to offer. The more you are able to genuinely receive from yourselves and others, the more you have to give.

Self Respect

A very popular female black singer, Aretha Franklin, is famous for belting out the song R-E-S-P-E-C-T! If you are always feeling taken for granted, unappreciated, or devalued by others, then it may be time to look at how you are disrespecting yourself by staying in relationships with them. When others in their own unconscious way do not treat you with respect, you can learn to give it to yourself. People treat you the way you *allow* them too!

Can you remember an example of a time when you were feeling really low, and then someone let you know that he or she really appreciated something about you? Can you remember how that made you feel? You can feel that glow of self-respect warming inside of you. You can feel the positive energy that it gives you. Self-respect may take some time to rebuild, especially if you have been criticized or verbally abused about your weight, your drinking or drug use.

Just say to yourself....I respect myself, if you don't (I don't care who you are) then it's *NEXT!* Sing it Aretha, *R-E-S-P-E-C-T!*

I will leave you with this final thought, *forgive yourself.* Just as you would forgive another if they made a mistake that hurt you, *forgive yourself*. Don't you deserve the graciousness of forgiveness for yourself that you extend to others? You need to look at your mistakes, learn form them, forgive, forget, and move on. You cannot go through life with a backpack of guilt draped on your back. Forgive... Forget...Move On. Live life one precious moment at a time.

"I am my own heroine."... Marie Bashkirtsell

Final Thoughts
Understanding Drug Abuse
and Addiction

Many people view drug abuse and addiction as strictly a social problem. Parents, teens, older adults, and other members of the community tend to characterize people, who take drugs as morally weak or as having criminal tendencies. They believe that drug abusers and addicts should be able to stop taking drugs if they are willing to change their behavior.

These myths have not only stereotyped those with drug-related problems, but also their families, their communities, and the health care professionals who work with them. Drug abuse and addiction compromise a public health problem that affects many people and has wide-ranging social consequences. This is NIDA's goal to help the public replace its myths and long-held mistaken beliefs about drug abuse and addiction with scientific evidence that addiction is a chronic relapsing and treatable disease.

Addiction does begin with drug abuse when an individual makes a conscious choice to use drugs, but addiction is not just "a lot of drug use." Recent scientific research provides overwhelming evidence that not only do drugs interfere with normal brain functioning creating powerful metabolism and activity. At some point, changes occur in the brain that can turn drug abuse into addiction, a chronic, relapsing illness. Those addicted to drugs suffer from a compulsive drug craving and usage and cannot quit by themselves. Treatment is necessary to end this compulsive behavior.

A variety of approaches are used in treatment programs to help patients deal with these cravings and possible avid drug relapse, NIADA research shows that addiction is clearly treatable. Through treatment that is tailored to individual needs patients learn to control their condition and live relatively normal lives.

Understanding drug abuse also helps in understanding how to prevent use in the first place, Results from NIDA (National Institute of Drug Addiction)-funded prevention research have show that comprehensive prevention programs that involve the family, schools, communities, and the media are effective in reducing drug abuse. It is necessary to keep sending the message that it is better to not start at all than to enter rehabilitation if addiction occurs.

Excerpted from www.recoveryzone.org/docs/articles.understanding-drug-abuse-and-addiction

Two Paths To Drug Use

"Research on the pathways to drug use and addiction suggest the immediate decision to use drugs is drive, basically one of two types of reasons. One group of young people seems to use drugs simply to feel good. They are seeking novelty or excitement, to have a good time. I include in this group those who say they use drugs just because all their friends are doing it: they just want to join in common fun or to be "cool." These kids are the ones most likely to be responsive to prevention programming that educates about the harmful effects of drugs on their bodies, and are most influenced by the powerful protective factor of having strong and loving parents interested and involved in all aspects of their lives. These kids also seem to have the best chances of being successfully taught to seek alternative ways of having fun and to resist the temptation to seek novelty in drugs and other harmful ways.

But there is also a second, very different group of young people who are using drugs for quite different, actually more intractable reasons. These are kids who in some way or another are suffering and use drugs to try to make themselves feel better or even normal. This group often includes people stuck in very difficult like situations- poverty or abusive families, for example. It also includes kids suffering from a variety of untreated mental disorders, like clinical depression, manic depressive illness, panic disorder, schizophrenia. Estimates are that as many as 10 million children adolescents may suffer from emotion and psychiatric problems of such magnitude that their ability to function is compromised, and the majority of those kids are at extremely high risk of becoming addicted to drugs. These young people are not using drugs to just feel good. These children are actually trying to medicate themselves with drugs, they use drugs because they think they will make them feel better, or normal, in the same way that other people might be given anti-depressants or anti-anxiety medications. The problem, of course, is that using illicit drugs is not an effective treatment. In addition to other, perhaps more obvious problems-like that their use interferes with normal functioning-this kind of drug use actually will ultimately make them feel worse, not better. Medical research has shown clearly that this kind of drug use only exacerbated underlying psychological problems.

Treatment Different For "Self-Medicators"

Both the preventive and the treatment approaches for these "self-medicating" young people need to be quite different from the approaches one would use with novelty seekers or social users. For example, it can't be very meaningful to warn people who feel terrible today that using drugs may alter their brains a month from now. Their problem is getting through today. Encouragement to seek alternative sources of fun or to seek nicer friends doesn't seem very meaningful for them either. Again, they are trying to get through today's issues.

Loree Taylor Jordan

Even the otherwise powerful protective factor of loving, supportive family involvement in the life of the child is not very effective in these areas. Those young people who are trying to self-medicate must have help with their underlying problems. They need professional treatment."
—Alan I. Leshner, Ph.D

Final Thoughts From Loree...The 3 C's

As I said in my opening chapter and throughout this book addiction is a treatable illness it is NOT moral weakness. If you see family a member, friend, boyfriend or girlfriend exhibiting some of this type of addictive behavior please understand that you cannot change them or love them out of their addiction. Remember the 3 C's...you did not Cause it, you can't Control it, and you certainly can't Cure it (their disease or behavior). This may be it a bitter pill to swallow but it is the cold hard truth.

Your best course of action is to run don't walk to seek help for yourself even though they have the disease. I say this because without help you will undoubtedly enable their behavior (i.e. lend money, bail them out, make excuses etc) by listening to their excuses, lies, manipulations and the most damaging of all believing all the promises of I will never do it again.... Remember they have a disease that they are unable to control! Their life is out of control! When they say I will never do it again i.e. get drunk, use drugs, gamble etc they really mean it...for the moment. Until the next compulsive wave of behavior takes over...let me explain it another way...their brain is broken! They will not under any circumstances make the right choice or decision without professional intervention or help no matter how much they love you, need you, and don't want to lose you. This may be hard to hear, but it is what you need to hear!

Remember earlier in this book I gave you the definition of insanity? Doing the same thing over and over and expecting a different result? Trust me you will become just as insane in your own behavior as the addict...checking up on them, following them, checking their cell phone, e-mails, and wallets if left to your own devices. Without help you will do this crazy behavior trying to control them and their addiction. It is predictable, it is insane and it is very unhealthy for you.

The best thing you can do is speak to a school counselor and check resources in this book to get help for yourself. Ask for assistance to come together with a professional and family members to stage an intervention by setting your boundaries of " I care about you" or " I love you" I am getting help for myself however if you don't get help our relationship, friendship or whatever is over. Remember the 3 C's!

Take good care of yourself you are worth it!

—Loree

There are really only two ways to approach life–as a victim or as a gallant fighter-and you must decide if you want to act or react, deal your own cards or play with a stacked deck. And if you don't decide which way to play with life, it always plays with you.
—Merle Shain

" It only takes one person to change your life–you "
—Ruth Casey

Resource Guide

For anyone struggling with an eating disorder

National Association of Anorexia Nervosa and Associated Disorders
P.O. Box 7 • Highland Park, IL 60035
Hotline: 1-847-831-3438 • www.anad.org/site/anadweb

National Eating Disorders Association
Informational and Referral Program
603 Stewart Street, Suite 803 • Seattle, WA 98101
1-800-931-2237 • www.nationaleatingdisorders.org

Overeaters Anonymous
A program of recovery
Overeaters Anonymous offers a program of recovery from compulsive overeating using the Twelve Steps and Twelve Traditions of OA. Worldwide meetings and other tools provide a fellowship of experience, strength and hope where members respect one another's anonymity. OA charges no dues or fees; it is self-supporting through member contributions.
World Service Office
505-891-2664 (USA) • www.oa.org

For anyone with a gambling problem

Gamblers Anonymous®
International Service Office
P.O. Box 17173 • Los Angeles, CA 90017
(213) 386-8789 • Fax (213) 386-0030 • www.gamblersanonymous.org

Harbour Point
Residential Gambling Rehab
Our Mission is: To provide a place of help and hope for problem gamblers and their families. We were conceived with the sole purpose of providing various levels of treatment and care to improve the everyday lives of those who have been adversely affected by gambling addiction and to help them make their lives manageable again.
Baltimore, MD
1800-Lost-bet • 1800-567-8238 • www.lostbet.com

Arnie & Sheila Wexler Associates
Arnie and Sheils Wexler, Certified Compulsive Gambling Counselors
Licensed Certified Alcohol and Drug Counselor,
213 Third Ave. • Bradley Beach, NJ 07720
888-LAST BET • www.aswexler.com

Friends or families of those with a gambling problem

Gam-Anon® International
Service Office, Inc.
PO Box 157 • Whitestone, NY 11357
718-352-1671 phone • 718-746-2571 fax • www.gam-anon.org

For anyone with a drug addiction problem

Narcotics Anonymous World Services, Inc.
PO Box 9999 • Van Nuys, California 91409 USA
Telephone (818) 773-9999 • Fax (818) 700-0700 • www.na.org

For friends and families of someone who has a drug addiction problem

Nar-Anon Family Group Headquarters, Inc.
22527 Crenshaw Blvd #200B • Torrance, CA 90505 USA
Telephone (310) 534-8188 or (800) 477-6291 • Fax (310) 534-8688
Email: naranonWSO@hotmail.com • www.nar-anon.org

For anyone with a drinking problem

Alcoholics Anonymous (AA) World Services, Inc.
475 Riverside Drive, 11th Floor • New York, NY 10115
212-870-3400
Alcoholics Anonymous® is a fellowship of men and women who share their experience, strength and hope with each other that they may solve their common problem and help others to recover from alcoholism. The only requirement for membership is a desire to stop drinking. There are no dues or fees for AA membership; we are self-supporting through our own contributions. AA is not allied with any sect, denomination, politics, organization or institution; does not wish to engage in any controversy, neither endorses nor opposes any causes. Our primary purpose is to stay sober and help other alcoholics to achieve sobriety.
www.aa.org
For more information, visit Alcoholics Anonymous at:
http://www.alcoholics-anonymous.org/?Media=PlayFlash

Friends and families of someone who has a drinking problem

Al-anon/Alateen
Al-Anon Family Group Headquarters, Inc.
1600 Corporate Landing Parkway • Virginia, Beach, VA 23454-5617
757-563-1600 • 1-888-4AL-ANON EST
www.Al-anonfamilygroups.org • www.al-anon.alateenorg

Other resources for drugs and alcohol

Stop Alcohol Abuse
www.stopalcoholabuse.gov

National Institute on Alcohol Abuse and Alcoholism (NIAAA)
Scientific Communications Branch
6000 Executive Blvd. Willco Building Suite 409 • Bethesda, MD 20892-7003
www.collegedrinkingprevention.gov

National Council On Alcoholism and Drug Dependence, Inc. (NCADD)
20 Exchange Place, Suite 2902 • New York, NY 10005
212-269-7797 • 800-NCA-CALL (24-hour affiliate referral)
www.ncadd.org

Mental health services

Substance Abuse & Mental Health Services Administration (SAMHSA)
1 Chole Cherry Road • Rockville, MD 20857
240-276-2420 • www.samhsa.gov

American Psychiatric Association (APA)
100 WilsonBlvd. Suite 1825 • Arlington, VA 22209
703-907-7300 • www.healthMinds.org

For further information visit the following sites:

Online article and resources
  • www.AddictionUniverity.com go to articles/lectures
  • www.southofboston.net/entreports/herion/day2.html
  • www.haolscan.com.comments/twalat/damage
  • www.drugfree.org/Portal/DrugIssue/MethResources/faces/index.html

To see the faces of meth
For real stories about the impact meth has had on people, visit
  • www.drugfree.org/Portal/DrugIssue/Meth/stories.html.

Office of National Drug Control Policy at
  • www.whitehousedrugpolicy.gov/drugfact/index.html

The Partnership for a Drug-Free America at
  • www.drugfree.org/
  • www.msnbc.com (http://www.msnbc.msn.com/id/3071772/), crystal meth
  • www.drugfree.org/Portal/DrugIssue/MethResources/faces/index.html to see the faces of meth.

For real stories about the impact meth has had on people, visit
  • www.drugfree.org/Portal/DrugIssue/Meth/stories.html.
  • www.drugabude.gov/about/welcome/aboutdrugabuse/

Alcohol and youth
  • www.nlm.nih.gov/medlineplus/alcoholandyouth.html

Alcohol consumption
  • www.nlm.nig.gov/medlineplus/alcoholconsumption.html

My Social Support System Adapted from Group Drug Counseling Participant
Recovery Workbook.
Holmes Beach, FL-Learning Publications, Inc. pp.15-17
  • www.coping.org/selfesteem/lifestyle/support.htm
  • www.nida.nih.gov/PDF/DCCA/GDCSession7.pdf

Use resources in your universities programs!

Loree Taylor Jordan has had to deal with Addictions as a Daughter and a Mother

Loree Taylor Jordan spent her childhood and teen years dealing with a raging alcoholic father who physically and verbally abused her, driving her into an addictive eating disorder to deal with her out of control emotions that destroyed her self-esteem.

Loree grew up and started a family of her own. Her life came full circle. She has weathered some exceedingly difficult times with her sons, both of whom have confronted serious addiction issues: Christopher is a recovering crystal meth drug abuser who has been in prison four times and is now in recovery. Brandon has also had his challenges with alcohol and drugs and went to rehab when he was 21.

Loree Taylor Jordan empowers college students whose uncertain self-image can be the foundation for addictions gaining momentum in their lives Ms. Jordan resonates with college students because she is approachable, down to earth, and authentic. With charismatic energy, and skill, Loree's heartfelt inspirational talks and effective solutions come from real life experience. Her action plan helps students overcome self-sabotage, become inspired to eagerly achieve goals and enhanced self-esteem.

She is so successful because she is so passionate about empowering others and truly speaks from her heart as a compassionate healer.

A recovering food addict herself, Loree's mission is clear: to help others recognize, understand and heal from unhealthy addictions as she has in her own life. Buoyed by the knowledge that addiction is not a moral failing but a disease, Loree determined that she must help educate others facing similar problems. Excelling as an advocate on health issues, Loree found her calling as an energetic and inspiring speaker and as a longtime radio host in the Bay Area, gaining widespread attention and hundreds of speaking engagements. Loree, was personally sought out by famed self-help guru Tony Robbins to be a guest speaker at his international Life Mastery Program.

Today, Loree has turned her attention to the scourge of addiction on college campuses where she is now bringing her message of non-threatening, non-judgmental advice to young audiences and educators in an effort to help thousands of people nationwide. She is the creator and founder of Addiction University bringing life saving information to college campuses across the nation.

Loree resides in the Bay Area with her husband, Frank. She is the mother of two grown sons, a stepdaughter and four grandchildren.

**Loree is available for speaking engagements and author interviews call
LTJ Associates, Inc.** • 877-24Loree • 245-6733 or 408-379-9488 or visit:
www.addictionUniversity.com
www.loreespeaksaboutaddiction.com